Best

Colas

MODERN WINEMAKING TECHNIQUES

BY
GLADYS BLACKLOCK

Published by
"The Amateur Winemaker Publications Ltd"
Andover, Hants.

First Edition 1982

ISBN 0 900841 71 0

Photographs by Arnold Jepson

Printed in Great Britain by
Standard Press (Andover) Ltd., South Street, Andover, Hants.

CONTENTS

ACKNOWLEDGEMENTS

My grateful thanks to my husband Joe, whose constant encouragement enabled this book to be written.

To my sister Doreen for finding the time in her very busy schedule to type the manuscript.

To all my evening class students over the last decade, whose questions and problems prompted me to look even further into the intricacies of winemaking techniques.

To Professor Gerry Fowles for allowing me to use his chemical data on Pectin and effects of freezing (Wine for all Seasons, No. 9. Straightforward Winemaking).

INTRODUCTION

In order to achieve a good, sound wine it is essential to prepare a perfectly balanced "must". A good must is achieved by balancing the additives with the extract obtained from the main ingredients. It therefore follows that a good extract is essential if the rest of the preparation and attention to detail is going to be of any use.

To achieve a good extract, various aids and means are at our disposal, and all recipe books for winemakers will recommend differing methods of preparing ingredients. These will depend on:

(a)   the author's preference;
(b)   the method considered most suitable for the ingredient; or
(c)   the style of wine being made.

This does not mean that any particular method is the right one or the wrong one. Each method used will produce a different type of extract resulting in different flavours in the finished wine. A classic example is apple wine. Steep the apples in cold water and the liquor will remain very light in colour with a fresh apple flavour. Steep the apples in hot water and the liquor is slightly more golden in colour and the flavour will be reminiscent of stewed apple, or apple pie.

A poorly made extract can only lead to a poor wine, giving on occasions a bad flavour, and sometimes a haze which is very difficult to clear.

Several factors have to be considered in preparing the extract, all of equal importance.

(a)   Spoilage yeasts and bacteria need to be destroyed;
(b)   Pectin has to be broken down;
(c)   Oxidation of natural flavours must be prevented.

Boiling in water is the obvious way to kill micro-organisms and is often described in many recipes. While still used in the preparation of some vegetable extracts, it is a method which ought to be avoided for other ingredients.

During the boiling process there will be an increase in soluble pectin and a loss of delicate flavour. Spoilage yeasts and bacteria are therefore best controlled by treating the juice or extract with sulphur dioxide before fermentation starts. A dose of 5 p.p.m. (i.e. one campden tablet or one 5 ml spoonful of 10% sodium metabisulphite stock solution) per gallon should be adequate.

Needless to say good, sound, ripe fruit will give a better extract than poor, bruised or decaying fruit. One needs to be very selective about "free" gifts, or very cheap, left-over fruit from market stalls, etc. Bruised apples and windfalls can be used by cutting off the damaged portions but an orange showing slight decay is of no use at all. The whole of the juice is often infected and will taste "off".

This book describes the different methods which can be used in order to extract the flavours and bouquets from our main ingredients, and by using the chart on page 104 for easy reference, the best methods for the ingredient and style of wine required can easily be understood.

The only way to achieve a perfectly balanced must is to make regular use of the hydrometer and acid testing kit. I therefore make no apology for including in this book, chapters on the use of the hydrometer and on measuring acidity. It is essential that these techniques are mastered and used regularly to achieve good quality wines.

Because this book is mainly concerned with flavour and fruit juice extraction, it dwells only briefly on the other very important aspects of the winemaking process, most of which are covered very adequately in other publications. However, it is very important that equipment is kept very clean and sterilised before and after use and the references to sulphite throughout the book indicate the use of a stock sulphite solution made up as follows:–

10% Stock Sulphite Solution
Stir 2 oz of sodium metabisulphite in one pint of boiling water until all is dissolved. Keep a small amount, about 5 fluid ounces, in a small bottle for sterilising the must or adding to finished wines, and the rest in a larger bottle for sterilising equipment, as the latter can be used many times over.

For sterilising equipment, pour some of the stock solution into the bucket and, using a J cloth, rub the whole of the inside of the bucket, the rims and lid, transferring the sulphite to the demijohn by means of the funnel. Rub the funnel well, inside and out, and shake the demijohn to ensure that the sulphite has adhered to the whole of the inside surface and transfer any remaining liquid back into the stock bottle. The wooden or plastic spoon and the nylon sieve can then be rubbed with the J cloth and any excess sulphite squeezed back into the stock bottle. Rub over the inside of the bucket once again with the J cloth to take up any excess moisture and your equipment is ready for use or storing until needed again.

One 5 ml spoonful = 1 Campden tablet = 5 p.p.m.

The solution will keep for 4–6 months.

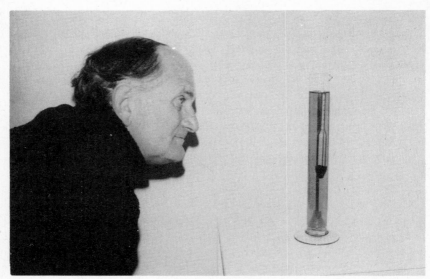

Hydrometer readings must be taken at eye level.

Chapter 1

THE HYDROMETER

The hydrometer is a piece of chemical apparatus that will measure the density, or specific gravity, of a liquid and to the keen winemaker it is probably the most important piece of his equipment.

Good wines can be made, and have been made many times in the past, without its use but these are usually wines made from set recipes where the quality of the ingredients does not vary unduly from year to year.

For the winemaker who wishes to be inventive in his winemaking and achieve style wines, dry and sweet, of a pre-determined alcoholic strength, the hydrometer must play a very important role.

It has been so designed that when floated in water at a given temperature it will read S.G. 1.000 (S.G. meaning specific gravity). Specific gravity is the weight of a given volume of liquid in relation to an equal amount of water in the same conditions.

As sugar is dissolved in the water, the hydrometer will float higher. The more dissolved sugar present the higher the hydrometer will float, the figures on the scale denoting the density or specific gravity of the liquid. At the opposite end of the scale, if alcohol is added to water, the hydrometer will sink lower in the liquid. This is because alcohol is less dense than water, pure ethyl alcohol having a specific gravity of 0.790.

Most hydrometers purchased by winemakers today have a scale ranging from 0.990 to 1.170 and have been designed for use in liquids at 70°F (21°C) but there are some available which have to be read at a temperature of 60°F (15°C). The temperature for which the hydrometer has been scaled is usually printed on it.

Because water expands and contracts as the temperature rises or falls, there will be a noticeable difference in the readings, as Chart I indicates. For this reason it is wiser to take readings at room temperature. However, occasionally it may be necessary to check the S.G. on wine taken directly from the cellar or before a must has cooled sufficiently, and in these cases adjustments to the readings should be made using the figures given in Chart I.

It is very important when purchasing a new hydrometer (and also to check the validity of those already in your possession) to ascertain if it reads correctly. The scale is usually on paper fixed inside the glass tube of the hydrometer and occasionally these have not been placed correctly or may in the course of time have come unstuck and slipped down the tube.

In order to check the correctness of your own hydrometer, place it in the test jar, or any tall glass jar that is suitable for the purpose, along with a thermometer and water. At the temperature recommended on the hydrometer scale it should float at exactly S.G. 1.000. On a recent check of my own hydrometers, which I have had for several years, three were correct and one read 1.004.

CHART I
Temperature Correction Factor

| Temperature | | Specific Gravity |
Cent	Fahr	correction
10	50	−0.001
15	59	None
20	68	+0.001
25	77	+0.002
30	86	+0.003
35	95	+0.005
40	104	+0.007

In the making of any wine, it is essential first to establish the amount of natural sugar in the must obtained from the ingredients.

In a juice fermentation this is relatively easy, but in a pulp fermentation more difficult. (See Chapters 4 and 5). Having diluted the fruit juice with water to the required amount, pour some into the test jar containing the hydrometer. A thermometer can be placed in the liquid to check when the temperature is correct. Note the level of the liquid against the scale when looking through the test jar at eye level, *not* by looking down from the top of the jar, and make a note of the S.G.

In a pure solution of water and sugar the specific gravity is constant but in a fruit juice other factors than the temperature have also to be taken into consideration. The presence of dissolved solids, organic acids, salts, pectins, etc., will affect the density of the liquid and give an increased S.G. In order to obtain a more correct reading it is necessary to subtract a figure of between 5 and 10, say 7 for an average must, to allow for the effects of these substances. e.g. A must whose recorded S.G. is 1.024 before any sugar addition would have a truer measurement due to natural sugar of 1.017 (approximately 8 oz natural per gallon).

Having ascertained the amount of natural sugar in the must, it is now possible to estimate the amount of sugar to add, bearing in mind that 1 lb sugar stirred into 1 gallon of liquid will raise the gravity by 36. It will also increase the volume of the liquid by a half pint. Similarly, 1 pint of grape concentrate will raise the gravity approximately 36. As most wines made need an addition of 2 lb sugar or more, it is preferable to start with approximately 7 pints of liquid to allow for the increase in volume.

The amount of sugar to add is governed by the wine type and Chart 2 gives an average assessment for most styles of wine. In some cases it is necessary to add further controlled amounts of sugar and Column 4 allows for this.

CHART 2

Wine Style	approx. A/V	approx. starting S.G.	further additional sugar	approx. finishing S.G.
Dry white table wine	11–12%	1.086	Nil	.992
Dry red table wine	12–14%	1.094	Nil	.990
Sweet white social wine	15–16%	1.100	½ lb	1.016
Sweet red social wine	15–16%	1.100	½ lb	1.016
White dessert wine	18%+	1.100	1 lb+	1.030–1.040
Red dessert wine	18%+	1.100	1 lb+	1.030–1.040
Dry aperitif wine	16–18%	1.100	Small amounts to finish dry.	.990 and below.

Yeasts will work at their best if the concentration of sugar is not too high. Whilst some books recommend that the initial S.G. should not exceed 1.130, it is preferable to start no higher than 1.100. Starting a fermentation with too much sugar can result in it stopping prematurely, leaving a very sweet wine of low alcohol content. More sugar can always be added during the fermentation to those wines where more alcohol is required.

The hydrometer is also useful for checking the progress of a fermentation. In dry wines, fermentation will normally be complete in 3 to 5 weeks, depending on the temperature maintained and the amount of alcohol being produced. All the sugar may be added at the beginning and the total volume and S.G. noted.

In pulp fermentation it is often advisable to add grape concentrate or grape juice after the fermenting liquid has been strained, so avoiding any being discarded with the pulp residue. Of course, this will mean taking two further hydrometer readings, the first after straining to note the S.G. and volume, and the second after the addition of grape concentrate or juice, to note the new S.G. and volume. Allowances must be made for this when preparing the must as the following example will show:

Example

Initial S.G. due to natural sugar	1.010	Approx 7 pints
1 lb 12 oz sugar added	1.074	
after straining	1.040	Volume 8 pints
½ pint concentrate added	1.058	Volume 8½ pints

The addition of ½ pint grape concentrate in 1 gallon of liquid raises the S.G. by 18 which equates to an approximate starting S.G. of 1.092.

In the making of dessert wines, it is essential to encourage the production of as much alcohol as possible and to this end it is necessary to add sugar in controlled amounts during the course of the fermentation.

The fermenting liquid should be put into a sterilised bucket each time an addition is necessary, the requisite amount of sugar added and stirred until dissolved and then replaced in the gallon jar. The jar should *not* be washed out at this stage as it is essential to maintain a good yeast colony.

A reading is taken before and after each addition and a record of the "drops" kept. The amount of sugar to add is governed by the S.G. reading each time and it is advisable to add only that amount of sugar which will ensure that the wine has the right degree of sweetness for drinking should the fermentation unexpectedly cease.

The following example is taken from my log book for Cherry and Bilberry Dessert Wine (Recipe – page 38)

		S.G.	drop	Volume
15.11.77	Fruit crushed. 2 pints boiling water added and when cool 1 teaspoonful pectolase			
16.11.77	Cold water added to 1 gallon (approx.)			
	S.G. for natural sugar	1.038		
	1¾ lb sugar added	1.092		
21.11.77	Strained	1.014	78	
	½ pint grape concentrate added	1.032		8 pints
26.11.77		1.000	32	
	1 lb sugar added	1.034		8½ pints
3.12.77		1.012	22	
	¾ lb sugar added	1.036		9 pints (approx)
22.12.77		1.032	4	
5.1.78	Racked	1.032		8¼ pints
24.3.78	Racked	1.032		
		Total drop	136	

Each time sugar is added the volume will increase and it may be necessary, having filled the gallon jar, to place any remaining liquid in a small bottle, remembering to add the contents of this bottle to the main brew each time a sugar addition is made.

13

Some books advocate that these additions should be made in the form of sugar syrup. Having carefully adjusted the must in the beginning, additions of water in the form of sugar syrup will increase the volume considerably, thereby reducing the acidity and body of the finished wine. Should this method of sugar addition be employed then more care will need to be taken in balancing the must to allow for the increase in volume.

Chapter 2

ACIDITY

A balanced acidity is essential to a wine and is the most important factor in its keeping properties. It gives freshness and brilliance to the finished wine and its presence is essential in fermentation.

All fruits contain some acid in varying quantities but grain, flowers and vegetables contain little or no acid at all. A fermentation conducted on a low acid must of below 2 p.p.t. as per sulphuric, may develop medicinal flavours that are impossible to eradicate.

The three main fruit acids are citric, malic and tartaric. Citric is the principal acid in oranges, lemons, grapefruit, elderberries, loganberries, raspberries and strawberries. Malic is the principal acid in apples, gooseberries, blackberries, cherries, damsons, peaches, rhubarb, plums, sloes and *unripe* grapes. Tartaric acid can only be found in any quantity in grapes and, of course, raisins and sultanas, which are dried grapes.

CITRIC ACID, as its name implies, is the main acid in citrus fruits and was the one most often used in the past by amateur winemakers. The old traditional recipes handed down from generation to generation always contained juice from oranges and lemons and it was an obvious choice, when acid became available in powdered form, to continue in this vein.

It is sharp, clean-flavoured, but is also the most susceptible to acetic bacteria.

When tasted in a water solution it has a faint lemon flavour.

MALIC ACID is a softer acid that is easily decomposed in heat. It is abundant in unripe grapes and can give a sour taste to a wine.

15

It is susceptible to lactic acid bacteria which can benefit an over-acid dry wine but is detrimental in a sweet wine.

It decomposes to lactic acid giving off carbon dioxide gas, leaving no sediment in the process (Malo-lactic fermentation).

However, in a sweet wine, lactic acid bacteria will also attack the sugar, converting it to mannitol which gives a bitter taste to the wine (MANNITIC fermentation). A sweet wine showing signs of a malo-lactic ferment should be dosed with sulphite to prevent this occurring and removed to a cooler place.

One other fault which may arise due to lactic acid bacteria is TOURNES disease causing ropiness or oiliness in the wine. Mousiness may also be attributed to this bacteria. When malic acid is tasted in a water solution it has a faint apple flavour.

TARTARIC ACID is a very stable acid which is more soluble in heat than in cold; the bitartrates becoming more insoluble with an increase in alcohol or a decrease in temperature.

The crystalline deposit settles on to the sides and bottom of the jar or bottles, reducing the acidity of the wine. This can be very useful if a wine is over-acid but can leave a wine too low in acid if it is stored over a long period in a cold cellar.

When tartaric acid is tasted in a water solution it has a "grapey" flavour.

ACIDS WHICH ARE BI-PRODUCTS OF FERMENTATION

1. *SUCCINIC ACID:* An acid produced during fermentation and allied to the amount of alcohol produced.

   i.e. A wine of 10% A/V will have 1% succinic acid present.
   A wine of 15% A/V will have 1.5% succinic acid present.

   It is an acid which aids bouquet, and full benefit is usually noticed after maturing for about 2 years.

   It can be purchased and added to wines intended for long keeping and is normally added at the first racking; the recommended amount being 3 grams per gallon.

   When tasted in a water solution it has a SALTY flavour.

2. *LACTIC ACID:* The result of the malo-lactic fermentation, it can also be bought in liquid form and can be useful for adding to a finished wine which is slightly deficient in acid.

3. *ACETIC ACID:* This is a volatile acid and a little is found in every wine but it should not be detectable on the palate.

The acetic acid found in some wines which are over old, or have been attacked by acetic bacteria, is a fault in a wine and is usually the result of bad winemaking practices.

Acetic acid tastes of vinegar.

4. *ASCORBIC ACID* or Vitamin 'C', is present is most fruits and acts as an anti-oxidant. In frozen fruit, most of the ascorbic acid is lost during the freezing process, so preventative measures have to be taken to prevent oxidation of the fruit juices.

It can be bought in Home Brew shops and may be used at the end of fermentation and before bottling as an anti-oxidant.

Over the years, the popularity of one acid over another has changed. Whilst citric acid may have been the first acid available to amateur winemakers, once the others were easily obtainable it became common practice to use a blend of the three main fruit acids, the blend depending on whether a dry or a sweet wine was being made.

It soon became apparent that, no matter which blend was chosen, the predominant acids in the fruit in the must were going to affect the acid blend in the finished wine.

The more discriminating winemakers made a note of the main acids in the fruit used and, should any acid addition be required to balance the must, would add the "missing" one.

For some years it has been the custom for many winemakers to use tartaric for all additions to musts deficient in acid. Being the main acid in ripe grapes and the one least susceptible to bacterial attack, it seems to be the most advantageous acid for use by winemakers. Its ability to tartrate out, thereby reducing the acidity of the maturing wine, can be allowed for in calculating acid additions at the beginning of fermentation, depending on storage conditions.

For instance, my own cellar has a winter temperature of no less than 46°F (8°C) which rises to 56°F (13°C) in the summer. A white grape table wine made in the autumn and placed in the cellar in November can lose .5 p.p.t. (measured as sulphuric) by April, a fine crystalline deposit forming on the bottom of the gallon jar. A similar wine made in early spring and placed in the cellar from April to November does not normally throw a tartrate and the acid remains stable.

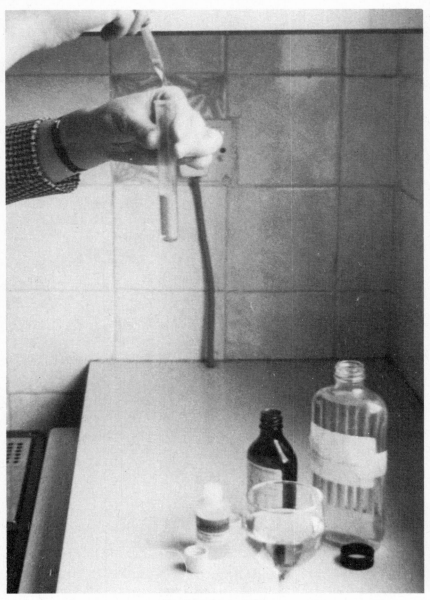

Testing for acidity.

18

To compensate for these conditions, white grape table wine is made .5 p.p.t. higher for wines made in the autumn for summer drinking.

The measurement of acidity in the must is an essential part of the good winemaker's technique so that the correct amount of acid can be added at the start of fermentation. There are several "aids" to winemakers to help in the assessment of acidity.

pH papers, available from most Chemists and Home Brew shops, are litmus papers which change colour when dipped into the wine or must. The resultant colour is compared with a colour chart supplied with the kit and the relevant pH noted. All wines should fall within the range of pH 3.0 to 3.4. This test is not accurate enough for the amateur winemaker as it gives no indication of the *total* acidity of the must or wine.

Possibly the least useful kit available provides litmus paper which, when dipped into the wine, has to be compared with just three colours on a chart marked LOW, MEDIUM or HIGH.

The best method of assessing *total* acidity is by titration and a very useful kit is available from most Home Brew shops at a very reasonable cost. It consists of a test-tube, a pipette graduated into 20 equal measures (m), a bottle of Sodium Hydroxide N10 and a bottle of phenol phthalein (acid indicator solution). A bottle of distilled water is also needed and this can be collected when defrosting the refrigerator.

METHOD: Fill the 20 m dropper with wine exactly to the mark, transfer to the test-tube, top up tube to approximately 1 inch (2 inches for a red wine) with distilled water, and add 3 to 4 drops of indicator solution. Rinse dropper tube in distilled water, then fill dropper tube with exactly 20 m sodium hydroxide. Add this to the test tube, drop by drop, swirling the contents to ensure mixing. The end point is reached when the colour changes to a faint but permanent pink.

Some highly acid wines will require more than 20 m sodium hydroxide and it will be necessary to fill the dropper again. Take the total amount of sodium hydroxide used and divide by 4, this will give the amount of acid in p.p.t. as per sulphuric.

e.g. Amount of sodium hydroxide used = 17 m ÷ 4 = 4.25 p.p.t.
The presence of carbon dioxide gas will affect the readings. To do a titration on a fermenting liquid, first place the test tube

containing the 20 m of must into a pan of boiling water for a few seconds until the gas has dispersed.

Sulphuric acid has been used as a standard for measuring total acidity in wines for many years and most wine books follow the same system. However, there are a few amateur winemaking books which have been written using tartaric or even citric as a standard. It is advisable that each person familiarises himself with one method and continues to use it to avoid confusion.

A chart is listed below showing conversion details for readers using alternative methods.

CONVERSION CHART

As per Sulphuric	As per Citric	As per Tartaric
3.0 p.p.t.	4.29 p.p.t.	4.59 p.p.t.
3.5 p.p.t.	5.01 p.p.t.	5.36 p.p.t.
4.0 p.p.t.	5.72 p.p.t.	6.12 p.p.t.
4.5 p.p.t.	6.44 p.p.t.	6.89 p.p.t.
5.0 p.p.t.	7.15 p.p.t.	7.65 p.p.t.

Wines vary in acidity according to type and once the initial acidity of the must has been assessed, acid is added to raise it to the correct amount required for its type. Generally speaking, white wines are more acid than red and sweet wines are more acid than dry. Following this principle the main styles of wine will have total acidities as follows:–

Dry Red Table Wine	3.0 –3.5 p.p.t. as sulphuric
Sweet Red Wine	3.25–3.75 p.p.t. as sulphuric
Red Dessert Wine	3.5 –4.0 p.p.t. as sulphuric
Dry White Table Wine	4.0 –4.5 p.p.t. as sulphuric
Sweet White Wine	4.25–4.75 p.p.t. as sulphuric
White Dessert Wine	4.5 –5.00 p.p.t. as sulphuric
Aperitifs	4.25–4.75 p.p.t. as sulphuric
Sparkling Wine	4.5 –5.00 p.p.t. as sulphuric

Using a 5 ml spoon, (the one usually issued by the Chemist with prescriptions for medicines) one level spoonful of acid will lift 1 gallon of liquid 0.5 p.p.t. One heaped teaspoonful will lift 1 gallon of liquid 1.0 p.p.t. A reasonably accurate heaped teaspoonful can be achieved by practise. Measure two level teaspoonfuls of acid into a cup and then scoop all on to the teaspoon and note the level.

There is very little difference in the strength of the three main acids, although citric acid will taste slightly sharper than the other two, so the same quantities suggested for tartaric acid additions may be used for either citric or malic. For those readers who are chemically minded and wish to have the exact data, the following will be useful.

Acid Addition to One Gallon of Must

Quantity	Citric	Malic	Tartaric
⅛ oz (1 level 5 ml spoon)	.54	.57	.51
¼ oz (1 heaped 5 ml spoon)	1.09	1.14	1.02
1 oz	4.37	4.56	4.07

An over acid must will produce an over acid wine so it is advisable to adjust the ingredients in the recipe at this stage.

Certain fruits, i.e. under-ripe green gooseberries, are very high in acid. These can make a very good dry table wine using only a small amount of fruit. Should a more full bodied wine of higher alcohol content and flavour be required, it is better to add another ingredient with little or no acid than increase the quantity of gooseberries. Elderflowers, lemon balm, oak leaves or vine prunings are useful ingredients to add to musts for table wines which are already sufficiently acidic.

Should an over acid wine still result, steps can be taken to reduce some of it. However, a wine which has just finished fermenting may still contain some dissolved carbon dioxide gas and as this will affect the reading it is advisable to wait until the wine is a few months old before doing anything decisive.

If tartaric acid was present in the must a little of this can be removed by placing the wine in a cold place such as the refrigerator for a few days. Any fall out of acid will appear as crystals on the bottom of the bottle. These are easily distinguishable from the normal sediment thrown in wine and are similar in appearance to sugar crystals.

Precipitated chalk and acid reducing solution can be used but only with caution. If too much is added it can affect the flavour of the finished wine. ½ oz chalk per gallon will reduce the acidity by about 1.5 p.p.t.

Acid reducing solution should be used according to the manufacturer's instructions. The average would appear to be approx 10 ml (½ fl oz) per gallon to reduce the acidity by 1.0 p.p.t.

Chapter 3

BODY AND VINOSITY

Whilst it is true to say that vinous ingredients in a must will also give body, it does not necessarily follow that ingredients added for body will also impart vinosity.

Quite often these two wine components are grouped together and some winemakers may be under the impression that they mean similar things. This is not so.

Body in a wine can be seen and can be felt. In other words, it is appreciated by two senses, the sense of sight and the sense of touch.

Vinosity is recognised in bouquet and in flavour, by the senses of smell and taste.

Body is apparent in wine in the glass by the way it clings to the sides of the glass when the wine is swirled. This can be due to the presence of alcohol, glycerine, and residual sugar in a sweet wine. Favourite descriptions of this appearance are "tears", "clinging well" or "legs in the wine". Whilst amateurs may say a wine is thin, has a good body, or is full bodied, the commercial imbiber may describe it as being light, heavy, fat, having a lot of fruit or having weight.

On the palate, the wine will *feel* full, will *feel* thicker. Body in wine, therefore, is basically due to its extract and alcohol content.

The degree of body required in a wine will vary according to the style of wine being made and guidance from commercial wines is not as clear as one would hope.

White, dry, table wines can range from very light in body, e.g. wines from the Moselle, to medium body, e.g. White Burgundies and Riojas. One would expect most red table wines to be medium in body, but they can be quite light as in some Beaujolais to fairly heavy as in some Rhône wines.

Dry fino sherry has not as much body as a dry white port yet they both have similar alcohol content.

The aim of the average winemaker should be to make wine with body in relation to its style so that the wine remains consistently in balance.

To generalise:–

Table wines should be light in body, red wines having more body than white.

Social wine should be medium in body.

Dessert wines should be heavy in body.

Aperitifs should be light to medium in body although containing as much alcohol as can be achieved by normal fermentation.

Fruits which are high in acid and need heavy dilution with water to reduce the acidity will obviously make thin wines unless other ingredients are added to make up the deficiency.

There are several low acid ingredients which can be used to increase the total fruit content of the must. Dates and bananas are both useful "body givers" but should be used sparingly. Dates may be added directly to the must, allowing ½ lb (250 grams) to the gallon.

Over-ripe black bananas may be used at the rate of 1 lb per gallon. More than this and a distinct banana flavour is detectable in the finished wine. The skins should be discarded and the bananas simmered in water for 15–20 minutes. The resultant liquid, which looks like dirty washing up water, can then be added to the must and the banana pulp thrown away.

Young oak leaves are a very useful additive to both white and red dessert style wines, two quarts being the equivalent of 1 lb of fruit. Wash the leaves in lightly sulphited water, cover with boiling water and leave to steep for 24 hours. Strain, keeping the water, turn the leaves over and cover again with boiling water. After a further 24 hours strain, discard the oak leaves and add the other ingredients and sufficient water to make 1 gallon.

Figs will also give body to a wine but they have a very strong flavour and should only be used in small quantities. Using only 3 oz (100 grams) per gallon, they combine very well with rosehips or parsnips to make sweet sherry style wines.

Prunes are a very useful additive in sweet red dessert style wines. After steeping over night in boiling water, they are simmered until tender, about 15–20 minutes, and the water added to the must. The cooked prunes can of course be used afterwards in a pudding.

According to the Oxford English Dictionary (shortened version) vinosity is "the flavour of wine, the quantity or state of being vinous".

Vinous has several definitions, among them:

(a) "of the nature of wine"
(b) "having the qualities of wine"
(c) "tasting and smelling of wine"
(d) "made or prepared with wine"

This does not really help the winemaker who has been advised that his wine lacks vinosity, or is not vinous. So perhaps we should look for a better explanation.

I prefer to think of vinosity or vinous as grapiness, or having grape qualities and for this reason it is essential that an ingredient specifically for this purpose is added to every wine made.

Raisins and sultanas are dried grapes and as well as giving vinosity to the wine will also improve the body. Raisins, however, range in colour from light brown to black and for this reason should not be used in white wines where it is important to preserve a light colour. There are several varieties of raisins on the market and one needs to be careful in choosing the right one for the style of wine.

Large muscatel raisins may be quite suitable in heavy dessert wines where the slightly cooked, madeirised flavour is acceptable, but they could spoil the flavour of a table wine. One particularly good variety of raisin for red table wine is the Shiraz raisin. It is a small, very black raisin and of the same grape variety as that used in the making of Rhône wines. Used on their own they can make a very good red table wine for early drinking. (See Recipe on page 40).

Most sultanas or raisins bought in polythene bags in supermarkets have been treated with oil to keep them moist and shiny and there is usually some wording on the wrapper to this effect. It is advisable to first wash the fruit carefully in running water and then, having covered with cold water, bring slowly to simmering point and strain. This will help to remove the oil from the skins of the fruit and also make them easier to chop or mince.

Recommended amounts are in the region of ½ lb to 1 lb (250–500 grams) per gallon depending on the style of wine being made.

Grape concentrates have been available for many years and there are several types available from Home Brew shops. A half pint of grape concentrate will give vinous character to a wine and an added sophistication is to use the correct grape concentrate for the required wine style, although this is not essential.

> e.g. A Riesling, Hock or Chablis style concentrate in a dry white table wine or a Burgundy or Claret style concentrate in a red table wine.

A half pint of grape concentrate is roughly equivalent in sweetness value to ½ lb sugar and allowances must be made for this in calculating sugar additions.

Unfortunately, some supposedly white grape concentrates are quite deep golden in colour and can darken an intended white table wine quite considerably.

During recent years I have made several gallons of wine from vine prunings and the flavour and bouquet have been sufficiently vinous for the wine to be mistaken for grape. Owing to the rising cost of grape concentrates and sultanas, I have made several batches of wine using vine prunings as a source of vinosity and they have been remarkably good.

Four separate gallons of Apricot and Orange wine (see Recipe on page 93) were made identical except for the ingredient for vinosity. This was added to each gallon of must in the following quantities:–

(a) ½ pint white grape concentrate
(b) 1 litre supermarket white grape juice
(c) ½ lb sultanas
(d) ½ lb vine prunings

Each gallon was then adjusted with sugar and tartaric acid to a starting gravity of 1088 and an acidity of 4.00 p.p.t. Each wine was dry at the end of fermentation. S.G. .990.

In a comparative blind tasting to spot the vinous ingredient, it was difficult to say which wine contained the vine prunings.

It is not necessary to own a green house in order to grow vines, even in the far north. We are successfully growing three vines outdoors (two Canadian Brandt and one Scheville Blanc) purely for the leaves. Whilst bunches of grapes do form, only in 1976 did they ripen sufficiently to make wine. The leaves and tendrils are gathered regularly during the summer, and in the autumn when the grapes are as ripe as they are ever likely to be, they are added also.

The vine prunings are treated in a similar manner to the method used for oak leaves, already described in this chapter, and the resultant liquid used as part of the water content for the brew.

A two gallon bucket when full of vine leaves, pressed down will hold approximately 3–3½ lb.

Pure grape juice, white and red, and free from preservatives, added sweetness and artificial colouring, is now readily available from most supermarkets and grocery stores. Recent tests on one brand showed an acidity of 4.25 p.p.t. as per sulphuric and a gravity of 66.

The addition of 1 litre in each gallon of must provides not only the necessary vinous character but increases the acidity and sugar content.

Preparing the pulp.

28

Chapter 4

PULP FERMENTATION

This is the method most often employed by amateur winemakers and resembles the old traditional method of winemaking used by our grandmothers and generations of winemakers before them.

The main ingredients are put into a bucket or other suitable container. Water is added, along with sugar, acid, tannin as necessary, possibly sultanas or raisins, nutrient and a pectin destroying enzyme. The bucket is suitably covered to protect the must from dust and invading flies and fermentation begins. During this stage of fermentation, the yeast is reproducing rapidly to build up a large colony of yeast cells and the must will rise to the surface forming a cap.

Stirring two or three times a day will break up the cap and ensure maximum extraction of flavour and the small amount of oxygen introduced into the must will aid in further yeast growth.

The period of time in the bucket can range from four to five days for most fruit wines and seven to ten days for cereal wines. At the end of this period the still fermenting liquid is strained through muslin or a nylon sieve into the demijohn and an airlock fitted. Maintaining a reasonable temperature (68–74°F or 20–22°C is ideal), the wine will continue to ferment for a further period and then slowly cease. Fermentation will have ceased either:

(a) because all of the sugar has been utilised by the yeast and converted into alcohol and carbon dioxide gas, and the wine will taste DRY, or

(b) the wine has varying degrees of sweetness because the yeast has reached its alcohol tolerance level, i.e. it is unable to ferment any further due to the presence of alcohol.

This then is a very basic description of fermentation and more information on this aspect of winemaking can be read elsewhere. This book is really concerned with the extraction of flavour and the ways and means to achieve the best results from the ingredients used.

Using the pulp fermentation technique several methods can be adopted to extract the necessary juice and flavour from the ingredients. Each method has its advantages and disadvantages depending on the ingredient and required wine style.

(i) Cold Soak

This is the method more often adopted for use with white fruits. The main ingredients are crushed, chopped or minced, put into a bucket with the requisite amount of cold water, and a 5 ml dose of sulphite added. The fruit is left to steep for about twenty four hours. At this point, it is customary in the making of most wines to take a hydrometer reading and do an acid titration to assess the natural sugar and acid content of the must.

Under these conditions any readings taken would be quite worthless as the sugar and acid would still be retained in the fruit.

Additions of sugar and acid, therefore, must be made to the must on the basis of previous attempts to make this wine or by following a tried and tested recipe. This will not always be successful. Unless identical fruit is used there will be variations in sugar and acid content. Climatic and soil conditions play a major part in the growth of fruit and vegetables, as gardeners well know. Gooseberries, apples, currants will vary in degrees of sweetness and acidity from one season to the next and are dependent on the climate as well as the gardener's expertise. The year 1976 will be long remembered as the year when our country fruits, elderberries, blackberries, rosehips, sloes, etc., ripened very early with a fairly high degree of sweetness and a less acid content than had been seen for years.

These are the variations which make it impossible to follow a set recipe year after year and a check for natural sugar and acid in our fruits is extremely important.

Oxidation and browning of the fruit surfaces can occur in some cases and it is advisable when making apple wine by this method to add the chopped apples to the sulphited water as a protective measure.

It is advantageous to use the cold soak method when making wines from cereals (barley, maize, rice or wheat). Hot water poured over these ingredients will release a certain amount of starch which could give rise to haze problems at a later stage. There being no natural sugar or acid in these ingredients, correct additions to the must can be made. It is not a good idea to crush the cereal as recommended in some recipes, as this again will only release starch, creating future haze problems. It is preferable to add the whole grain (suitably washed of course) and obtain the flavour from the outer husk only. Being a hard shell, a longer period of pulp fermentation is necessary to obtain the required flavour and quite often fermentation will have ceased on transferring to the demijohn. More sugar can of course be added, either to continue the fermentation or to make a sweet wine.

Gooseberry and Orange
(dry white table wine)

Ingredients to make 1 gallon (4.5 litres)

1½ lb (750 grams) green gooseberries
Juice of 6 oranges
½ pint (300 ml) white grape concentrate
1 teaspoonful pectin destroying enzyme
1¾ lb (875 grams) sugar
1 teasp. yeast nutrient
1 x 3 mg Vitamin B1 tablet
Yeast starter (Chablis, Bernkasteller or General Purpose)

Method:

Crush the washed gooseberries into a fermentation bucket and add the orange juice, grape concentrate and sugar. Add cold water to 1 gallon (4.5 litres), the pectin destroying enzyme and yeast nutrient, stirring until the sugar is dissolved. Add active yeast starter. No acid is necessary as the main ingredients are usually sufficiently acidic to give a titration of approx. 4.5 p.p.t. Stir 2 or 3 times daily for 4–5 days and then strain into gallon jar, adding the Vitamin B1 tablet. Ferment in the normal manner, racking when fermentation has ceased.

The yeast starter bottle

Apricot and Orange (dry white wine)

Ingredients to make 2 gallons (9 litres)

2 x 14 oz cans half apricots
1 litre unsweetened orange juice
2 teaspoonfuls pectin destroying enzyme
2 kilos sugar
2 teaspoonfuls yeast nutrient
2 x 3 mg Vitamin B1 tablets
5 rounded teaspoonfuls tartaric acid
1 teaspoonful Kwik-Sol Bentonite (optional)
Active yeast starter (Chablis, Johannisberger or General Purpose)

32

Method:

Put fruit and sugar into bucket and add water to 2 gallons (9 litres) pectin destroying enzyme, Bentonite, acid and yeast nutrient, stirring till sugar is dissolved. Add active yeast starter. Stir 2 or 3 times daily for 4–5 days and then strain into 2 x 1 gallon jars adding 1 Vitamin B1 tablet to each jar. Ferment in the normal manner, racking when fermentation has ceased. This wine is very clear and drinkable in 6 weeks.

The addition of Bentonite speeds up the clearing process.

Apple (dry white wine)

Ingredients to make 1 gallon (4.5 litres)

6 lb (2.75 kilos) apples (mixture of cooking and eating apples – a few crab apples may be included if wished)
½ lb (250 g) sultanas (washed and chopped)
2 lb (1 kg) sugar
1 teaspoonful yeast nutrient
1 teaspoonful tartaric acid
1 x 3 mg Vitamin B1 tablet
1 teaspoonful pectin destroying enzyme
1 Campden tablet or 5 ml sulphite solution
Active yeast starter (Chablis or General Purpose)

Method:

Prepare the fermentation bucket with approx. 6 pints (3.4 litres) cold water, acid and 5 ml sulphite solution. Wash the apples thoroughly in cold water, cut each into small pieces and put immediately into the prepared sulphited water. Add the sultanas, the pectin destroying enzyme, yeast nutrient and active yeast starter. Turn the fruit over two or three times daily for 4–5 days, preferably by hand as the quantity of fruit will make stirring difficult. It is also possible to hand squeeze the fruit each time to assist in juice extraction. Strain and press the apple pulp to extract as much juice as possible. Add sugar and Vitamin B1 tablet. Stir till sugar is dissolved and transfer to gallon jar. Ferment in the normal manner, racking when fermentation has ceased.

Orange (sweet white wine)

Ingredients to make 1 gallon (4.5 litres)

12 large oranges
8 oz (250 grams) packet dates
8 oz (250 grams) washed and chopped sultanas
½ pint (300 ml) white grape concentrate
2 lb (1 kg) sugar
2 teaspoonfuls tartaric acid
1 teaspoonful pectin destroying enzyme
1 teaspoonful yeast nutrient
1 x 3 mg Vitamin B1 tablet
Active yeast starter (Sauternes or General Purpose)

Method:

Juice the oranges and thinly pare the rinds of six of them, using a potato peeler to avoid the pith. Put the juice and the rinds into a fermentation bucket with the dates and sultanas. Add 6 pints (3.4 litres) of cold water, the sugar, acid and pectin destroying enzyme and stir till the sugar is dissolved. Add nutrient and active yeast starter. Stir 2 or 3 times daily for 4–5 days and then strain. Add grape concentrate and Vitamin B1 tablet and transfer to gallon jar. Add a further ½ lb (250 g) sugar after 1 week and make another addition of sugar if necessary for the wine to finish sweet – S.G. 1020 approx. Rack when fermentation has ceased in approx. 4–5 weeks from the start of fermentation.

34

Rice and Raisin (dry white wine)

Ingredients to make 1 gallon (4.5 litres)

1½ lb (750 g) white pudding rice
1 lb (500 g) raisins washed and chopped
2½ lb (1.25 kg) sugar
1 orange
½ pint (300 ml) white grape concentrate
2 heaped teaspoon tartaric acid
1 teaspoonful nutrient
1 Vitamin B1 tablet (3 mg)
Active yeast starter (General Purpose)

Method:

Put the raisins, sugar and rice into a sterilised bucket and add 7 pints cold water. Stir until the sugar is dissolved and add the orange rind, cut thinly to avoid the pith, orange juice, acid, nutrient and active yeast starter. Stir 2 or 3 times daily for 8–10 days then strain. Add the grape concentrate, Vitamin B1 tablet and transfer to a gallon jar under an airlock. Rack when fermentation has ceased and the wine is dry. (S.G. .990 approx.)

Orange and Wheat (dry white wine)

Ingredients to make 1 gallon (4.5 litres)

1 lb (500 g) wheat
Juice and rinds of 6 oranges
2½ lb (1.25 kg) sugar
½ lb (250 g) sultanas washed and chopped
1 heaped teaspoon tartaric acid
1 teaspoonful nutrient
1 Vitamin B1 tablet (3 mg)
Active yeast starter (General Purpose)

Method:

Put the sultanas, sugar and wheat into a sterilised bucket and add 7 pints cold water. Stir until the sugar is dissolved and add the orange rinds, cut thinly to avoid the pith, orange juice, acid, nutrient and active yeast starter. Stir 2 or 3 times daily for 8 to 10 days then strain. Add a further ½ lb (250 g) sugar and stir till dissolved. Transfer to a gallon jar under airlock adding a Vitamin B1 tablet. Rack when fermentation has ceased and the wine is dry. (S.G. .990 approx.)

(ii) Hot Soak

This method is often used in the making of wine from red fruits. Boiling water is poured over the crushed fruit. 5 ml sulphite added, stirred and then left to steep for twenty four hours. By using hot water a good colour extraction is more quickly obtained and most of the natural acid and sugar will be released into the liquid. It is possible to take reasonably accurate hydrometer and titration readings at this stage and make the correct additions for the intended style of wine.

By steeping in hot water, the soluble pectin level of the fruit juice will increase and protective measures need to be taken to prevent haze problems later on. It is advisable to add a pectin destroying enzyme (pectinol, pectolase, pectinex) to every fruit must before fermentation begins at the rate of one teaspoonful per gallon but where hot water has been used in the preparation, two teaspoonfuls would be more in order. Pectinex is a much stronger preparation and one should follow the manufacturer's instructions.

Fermenting for too long on the pulp can give a bitterness and hardness to the finished wine. The little seeds in blackberries can be quite bitter and the skins of elderberries contain large amounts of tannin. Fermenting on these fruits for lengthy perods will extract flavours and tannins to an excessive degree and the resultant wine will take longer to mature. A pulp fermentation of four to five days is quite sufficient and the maximum extraction of flavour required should have been obtained in that time.

Cherry and Sloe (sweet red wine)

Ingredients to make 1 gallon (4.5 litres)

5 lb (2.3 kg) morello or dark red cherries
½ lb (250 g) dried sloes
8 oz (250 g) packet dates
½ lb (250 g) washed and chopped sultanas
½ pint (10 fl oz) (300 ml) red grape concentrate
2 lb (1 kg) sugar to start
1 teaspoonful tartaric acid
2 teaspoonfuls pectin destroying enzyme
1 teaspoonful yeast nutrient
1 x 3 mg Vitamin B1 tablet
Active yeast starter (Tarragona or Madeira)
1 Campden tablet or 5 ml sulphite solution

Method:

Crush the cherries in fermentation bucket, add sloes, dates and sultanas and 1 Campden tablet and cover with 6 pints (3.5 litres) boiling water. Leave for 24 hours. Add sugar, acid and pectin destroying enzyme and stir till sugar is dissolved. Add yeast nutrient and active yeast starter. Stir 2 or 3 times daily for 4 to 5 days removing any loose stones which rise to the surface of the fermenting must. Strain, add grape concentrate and Vitamin B1 tablet and transfer to gallon jar. Add more sugar as necessary whenever the gravity drops to S.G. 1.010 finishing with an S.G. of 1.020. Rack when fermentation has ceased. If a reasonable temperature has been maintained this will be about 5–6 weeks from the start of fermentation.

Cherry and Bilberry
(sweet red wine (dessert style))

Ingredients to make 1 gallon (4.5 litres)

2 x 2 lb (936 g) jars bottles cherries
1 x 1½ lb (680 g) jar bottled bilberries
8 oz (250 g) packet dates
8 oz (250 g) washed and chopped raisins
2 lb (1 kg) sugar to start
1 teaspoonful tartaric acid
1 teaspoonful tannin
2 teaspoonfuls pectin destroying enzyme
1 teaspoonful yeast nutrient
1 x 3 mg Vitamin B1 tablet
½ pint (300 ml) red grape concentrate
Active yeast starter (Madeira or Tarragona)

Method:
Put the total contents of bottled fruit into the fermentation bucket and crush. Add dates, raisins and pour over 6 pints (3.5 litres) boiling water. When cool add sugar, acid, tannin, pectin destroying enzyme and stir till sugar is dissolved. Add yeast nutrient and active yeast starter. Stir 2 or 3 times daily for 4–5 days removing any loose cherry stones which may rise to the surface. Strain, add grape concentrate and Vitamin B1 tablet and transfer to gallon jar. Add additional sugar as necessary each time the gravity drops to S.G. 1.010 finishing with a final S.G. of 1.030. Rack when fermentation has ceased. If a reasonable temperature has been maintained this will be about 5–6 weeks from the start of fermentation.

Shiraz Raisins (dry red table wine)

Ingredients to make 1 gallon (4.5 litres)

- **2 lb (1 kg) Shiraz raisins**
- **2 lb (1 kg) sugar**
- **1 campden tablet**
- **1 heaped teaspoon tartaric acid**
- **1 teaspoonful nutrient salts**
- **1 Vitamin B1 tablet (3 mg)**
- **1 teaspoonful pectolase**
- **Active yeast starter (Burgundy or Bordeaux)**

Method:

Wash the raisins in cold water, put them into a pan with enough cold water to cover them and bring to simmering point. Strain the liquid into a sterilised bucket, chop or mince the raisins and add them to the strained liquid with 1 campden tablet, sugar and sufficient hot water to make 1 gallon (4.5 litres). After 24 hours add the acid, pectolase, nutrient and active yeast starter. Stir 2 or 3 times daily for 4 to 5 days. Strain into gallon jar adding the Vitamin B1 tablet and fix an airlock.

Fermentation should be complete and the wine dry (S.G. 990) within 3 to 4 weeks when the wine should be racked. It will clear very quickly and can be drunk after the second racking at about 6 to 8 weeks old.

Rosehip and Fig (sweet golden/tawny wine)

Ingredients to make 1 gallon (4.5 litres)

- **6 oz (200 g) dried Rosehip shells**
- **3 oz (100 g) dried figs**
- **½ lb (250 g) washed and chopped sultanas**
- **½ pint (300 ml) white grape concentrate**
- **2 lb (1 kg) sugar**
- **1 campden tablet**
- **1 heaped teaspoonful tartaric acid**
- **1 teaspoonful pectolase**
- **1 teaspoonful nutrient**
- **1 Vitamin B1 tablet (3 mg)**
- **Active yeast starter (Tokay or Madeira)**

Method:

Wash the figs in cold water, cut them into small pieces and place in a large basin with 1 pint (550 ml) boiling water. When cool add the active yeast starter. Put the rosehip shells, sultanas and sugar into a sterilised bucket with 5 pints (2.5 litres) boiling water and add 1 campden tablet. Stir and leave to soak for 24 hours.

Strain the fermenting fig liquid on to the rosehip must, keeping the figs for further use in the kitchen, and add acid, pectolase and nutrient. Stir in grape concentrate, Vitamin B1 tablet and transfer to gallon jar under airlock.

The wine should be fed with additional sugar as necessary each time the hydrometer reading drops to S.G. 1.010 approximately. When fermentation ceases, rack, sweetening if necessary for a finishing gravity of 26 to 30.

Damson (sweet red wine (dessert style))

Ingredients to make 1 gallon (4.5 litres)

6 lb (3 kg) damsons
1 lb (500 g) washed and chopped raisins
½ lb (350 g) dates
2 lb (1 kg) sugar
½ pint (300 ml) red grape concentrate
1 heaped teaspoon tartaric acid
1 teaspoonful pectolase
1 teaspoonful nutrient
1 Vitamin B1 tablet (3 mg)
Active yeast starter (Madeira, Tarragona or General Purpose)

Method:

Wash and stone the damsons and put into a sterilised bucket with the raisins, dates and sugar. Add 7 pints boiling water and stir until the sugar is dissolved. When cool add the acid, pectolase, nutrient and active yeast starter. Stir 2 or 3 times daily for 4–5 days then strain. Add the grape concentrate and a further ½ lb (250 g) sugar stirring until the sugar is dissolved. Add Vitamin B1 tablet and transfer to a gallon jar under airlock.

Further additions of sugar may be added as necessary while the wine is fermenting, the final addition being made at the first racking to give the desired degree of sweetness (S.G. 1.026–1.030).

Peach (sweet white wine (dessert type))

Ingredients to make 1 gallon (4.5 litres)

4 lb (2 kg) peaches
8 oz (250 g) packet dates
½ lb (250 g) sultanas washed and chopped
½ pint (300 ml) white grape concentrate
2 lb (1 kg) sugar to start
2 teaspoonfuls tartaric acid
2 teaspoonfuls pectin destroying enzyme
1 teaspoonful yeast nutrient
1 x 3 mg Vitamin B1 tablet
Active yeast starter (Chateau d'Yquem, Sauternes or Tarragona)
1 Campden tablet or 5 ml sulphite solution

Method:

Stone the peaches and put into fermentation bucket with dates and sultanas. Add Campden tablet and 6 pints (3.5 litres) boiling water and leave for 24 hours. Add sugar, acid and pectin destroying enzyme and stir till sugar is dissolved. Add yeast nutrient and yeast starter. Stir 2 or 3 times daily for 4–5 days, then strain, adding grape concentrate and Vitamin B1 tablet and transfer to gallon jar. Add sugar each time the gravity drops to S.G. 1.010, making the final addition when fermentation has ceased to raise the finishing gravity to S.G. 1.030.

(iii) Alcohol Extraction

Very well known to those winemakers who have made liqueurs by the infusion method, the principle is easily adaptable for the production of some wines.

In the making of Sloe or Damson gin, fruit, sugar and alcohol (in this case gin) are put into a jar and the lid screwed tightly down. The jar is shaken frequently over a period of six to eight weeks and then strained. The gin has absorbed flavour and colour from the fruit and the result is a very nice fruit liqueur.

In the making of draught beer, in some breweries it is the custom to "dry hop" the beer to impart a more hoppy aroma before leaving the brewery, working on the principle that the alcohol already present will extract further flavour and bouquet from the fresh hops.

Winemakers of many years standing will remember the old fashioned method of making "Marrow Rum". The top is sliced off a large marrow, the seeds scooped out and then the marrow is stuffed with brown sugar. After adding yeast it is placed in a muslin bag and suspended over a bucket. During the following few days, the yeast works on the sugar and marrow flesh and the resulting liquid seeps into the bucket. When all the sugar and the fleshy part of the marrow have disintegrated and seeped through, the liquor is made up to one gallon with water, acid and nutrient added and fermentation continued in the normal manner. The alcohol being produced and of course the sugar, extracts the juices from the marrow.

This method of extracting flavour and bouquet can be used to great advantage in the making of wines from flowers where the bouquet is the most important feature in the wine. Prepare a must containing water, sugar, acid and something for vinosity (sultanas or grape juice) and add the nutrient and active yeast starter. After three to four days gather the flowers from the hedgerow or garden on a fine, sunny day where possible, and add them to the fermenting liquid.

The alcohol already present will destroy any micro-organisms on the blossom and will extract the colour, flavour and bouquet very quickly, usually within a further two to three days.

42

Using this method, the delicate flavours and bouquets of the flowers are preserved. The only flowers that should be subjected to boiling water are the dandelion and burnet, as this appears to be the best method for these particular flowers. There being no acid and virtually little sugar in the flower petals, the must can be perfectly balanced before fermentation begins.

Peach and Lemon Balm (dry white wine)

Ingredients to make 1 gallon (4.5 litres)

4 lb (2 kg) fresh peaches
½ pint (300 ml) lemon balm leaves
1 litre bottle white grape juice
2 teaspoonfuls tartaric acid
2 teaspoonfuls pectin destroying enzyme
2 lb (1 kg) sugar
1 x 3 mg Vitamin B1 tablet
1 teaspoonful yeast nutrient
Active yeast starter (Johannisberger, Riesling, General Purpose)
1 Campden tablet or 5 ml sulphite solution

Method:

Put the stoned peaches into a fermentation bucket with grape juice and 1 Campden tablet. Leave for 24 hours, add sugar, acid, pectin destroying enzyme and water to 1 gallon (4.5 litres) and stir till sugar is dissolved. Add nutrient and yeast starter and stir daily for 2 days. Add lemon balm leaves and stir 2 or 3 times daily for a further 2–3 days and then strain into gallon jar, adding Vitamin B1 tablet. Ferment in the normal manner, racking when fermentation has ceased.

Juniper and Tea (dry white wine (aperitif style))

Ingredients to make 1 gallon (4.5 litres)

2 oz (60 g) tea (Jasmine or orange flavoured Peeko)
1 oz (30 g) dried Juniper berries
½ lb (250 g) washed and chopped sultanas
Juice and thinly peeled rind of 1 orange
2 lb (1 kg) sugar
3 heaped teaspoons tartaric acid
1 teaspoonful nutrient
1 Vitamin B1 tablet (3 mg)
Active Yeast starter (Cold Fermentation or General Purpose)

Method:

Infuse the tea leaves in 7 pints (4 litres) of boiling water and leave till the tea is "brewed". Strain over the sugar and sultanas in a sterilised bucket and stir till the sugar is dissolved. When cool add acid, orange juice, nutrient and active yeast starter. Put the orange rind and juniper berries into a basin, cover with boiling water and leave to steep for 24 hours. Add (liquid and fruit) to the must when it is actively fermenting. Stir 2 or 3 times daily for 4–5 days then strain. Add a further ½ lb (250 g) sugar and the Vitamin B1 tablet and transfer to a gallon jar under airlock.

Additional sugar may be added as necessary during the fermentation in order to achieve the maximum amount of alcohol but the wine should finish dry. (S.G. .990 or below). To achieve this, sugar should be added in small amounts (2 to 3 oz) (60–100 g)) as the S.G. drops to 1.000 and the last addition made whilst the wine is still fermenting to ensure a dry finish.

Philadelphus (Mock Orange Blossom) (dry white wine)

Ingredients to make 1 gallon (4.5 litres)

2 quarts (2.25 litres) Philadelphus petals
½ lb (250 g) washed and chopped sultanas
2½ lb (1.25 kg) sugar
3 heaped teaspoonfuls tartaric acid
1 teaspoonful nutrient
1 Vitamin B1 tablet (3 mg)
Active yeast starter (General Purpose)

Method:

Put the sultanas and sugar into a sterilised bucket with 1 gallon (4.5 litres) boiling water. Stir until the sugar is dissolved and when cool add the acid, nutrient and active yeast starter. When the must is actively fermenting add the fresh gathered petals. Stir 2 or 3 times daily for 4 to 5 days then strain into a gallon jar under airlock adding the Vitamin B1 tablet. Extra sugar may be added as necessary during fermentation if a sweet wine is desired. Rack when fermentation has ceased in 3 to 5 weeks.

Coltsfoot and Tea (dry white wine)

Ingredients to make 1 gallon (4.5 litres)

2 oz (60 g) tea (preferably an orange flavoured Peeko or Earl Grey)
2 oz (60 g) dried coltsfoot flowers
½ lb (250 g) washed and chopped sultanas
3 heaped teaspoons tartaric acid
2 lb (1 kg) sugar
1 teaspoonful nutrient
1 Vitamin B1 tablet (3 mg)
Active yeast starter (General purpose)

Method:

Scald the tea with 1 gallon (4.5 litres) of boiling water. When fully mashed, strain, add the sultanas, sugar and acid and stir till the sugar is dissolved. When cool, add nutrient and active yeast starter. When the must is actively fermenting add the coltsfoot flowers. Stir 2 or 3 times daily for 3 to 4 days, strain, add ½ lb (250 g) sugar and Vitamin B1 tablet and transfer to gallon jar under an airlock. When fermentation has ceased (3 to 5 weeks) rack. If a sweet wine is required add additional amounts of sugar as necessary during fermentation to finish at approximately S.G. 1.016–1.020.

Rosepetal Wine (dry rosé wine)

Ingredients to make 1 gallon (4.5 litres)

2 quarts (2.25 litres) Rose petals (white, yellow and red)
2 pints (1 litre) red grape juice
2½ lb (1.25 kg) sugar
3 heaped teaspoonfuls tartaric acid
1 teaspoonful nutrient
1 Vitamin B1 tablet (3 mg)
Active yeast starter (General Purpose)

Method:

Sterilise the fermentation bucket and add grape juice, sugar, acid and water to make 1 gallon (4.5 litres). Stir till the sugar has dissolved and add nutrient and active yeast starter. When it is fermenting vigorously, add the freshly gathered rose petals. Stir 2 or 3 times daily for 4 to 5 days, then strain into a gallon jar under airlock adding the Vitamin B1 tablet. Additional sugar may be added as necessary during fermentation if a sweet wine is required.

Rack when fermentation has ceased in 3 to 5 weeks.

Elderflower and Gooseberry (medium dry white table wine)

Ingredients to make 1 gallon (4.5 litres)

1½ lb (750 g) green gooseberries
½ pint (300 ml) Elderflower petals
2 lb (1 kg) sugar
½ pint (300 ml) white grape concentrate
Tartaric Acid as necessary (none required in test recipe as gooseberries sufficiently acidic)
1 teaspoonful pectolase
1 teaspoonful nutrient
1 Vitamin B1 tablet (3 mg)
Active yeast starter (Riesling or Johannisberger)

Method:

Cover the gooseberries in a little hot water and 1 Campden tablet and leave for 24 hours to soften. Crush and add sugar and cold water to 1 gallon (4.5 litres). Stir till the sugar is dissolved and add acid if required to 4.5 p.p.t., pectolase, nutrient and active yeast starter. Stir 2 or 3 times daily and when actively fermenting add the freshly gathered elderflower petals. Strain after a further 3 days, add grape concentrate and Vitamin B1 tablet and transfer to a gallon jar under an airlock. Rack when fermentation has finished in 3 to 4 weeks, and the wine medium dry. (S.G. 1.000–1.004 if a lighter style German yeast has been used.)

Maceration carbonique in a sweet jar.

(iv) Maceration Carbonique

This unusual and not very widely known method of fermentation is to be found in the Beaujolais and Midi districts of France. Whole bunches of grapes, including stalks, are put uncrushed into a vat which is then filled with carbon dioxide gas. Fermentation starts *inside* each grape extracting colour from the skin internally, and eventually, due to the pressure of gas and weight of fruit, bursting the berries. The fruit will remain in the sealed vat for about four to five days after which time it is crushed and transferred to a further vat to complete its fermentation. This process produces a wine of good colour, very fruity and soft, which is ready for early drinking.

In the hands of the amateur, this sounds a dangerous technique to follow, but it has been successfully tried using containers more available and suitable to the amateur winemaker.

Method 1 makes use of a plastic sweet jar with wide neck and plastic screw lid obtainable free of charge from confectioners' shops.

The jar is thoroughly cleansed and sterilised and filled with fruit. It will normally hold about six to seven pounds depending on the type of fruit used. Add a half pint of active yeast starter, screw the plastic lid down tightly and leave to ferment for seven days in a polythene bucket with a fitted lid. Fermentation of the fruit sugar will soon begin and the fruit will rise in the jar.

At the end of the seven day period, the contents are transferred to a fermentation bucket, water, sugar and the other necessary ingredients added and left for a further two days before straining and continuing the fermentation in the normal manner.

It sounds simple but the build up of carbon dioxide gas in a closed polythene container would appear to pose a major problem, the fear of the 'seams' of the container splitting under the pressure. However, in practise an occasional 'burp' is heard which seems to indicate that the lid of the container is so ill-fitting as to allow an escape of gas.

Method 2 is conducted in a pressure cooker. The pressure cooker is lined with a large, strong polythene bag and filled with fruit to the level one would normally use in cooking. A half pint of active yeast starter is added, the lid fitted, using the 15 lb weight, and left for seven days, again at a temperature of 65–70°F (19–21°C). This is a more ideal method as the pressure of carbon dioxide gas is more strictly controlled. It is essential that a strong polythene bag is used inside the pressure cooker, firstly as a preventative measure against seepage of fermenting liquid into the pan and also to enable easier removal to a fermentation bucket.

Both methods produce pleasant wines which are soft on the palate and ready for drinking in a few weeks. Gooseberries processed in this manner remained whole throughout. After transferring to the bucket they were very soft and it was easy to squeeze them by hand to express the carbon dioxide gas. After a further two days in bucket with the water and other ingredients they were pressed again and although the juice had now been extracted the berries still appeared to be whole without any noticeable breaks in the skins.

The main 'snag' is the inability to check for natural sugar and acid at the start of the fermentation so additions of these ingredients must be made on the basis of previous known qualities of the fruit used.

Gooseberry and Orange (dry white table wine)

Ingredients to make 3 gallons (13.5 litres)

6 lb (2.75 kilos) green gooseberries
1 carton (6¼ fl oz 178 ml) Bird's Eye Florida Orange Juice
2 litres white grape juice
6½ lb (3 kilos) sugar
Pectin destroying enzyme
3 x 3 mg Vitamin B1 tablets
3 grams Kwik-Sol Bentonite (optional)
1 teaspoonful yeast nutrient
½ pint (10 fl oz 300 ml) yeast starter (Chablis, Johannisberger)

Method:

Place washed gooseberries into container, add ½ pint (300 ml) yeast starter and seal. Stand in a warm place and leave to ferment for seven days. Transfer to sterilised bucket and add water to approximately 2½ gallons (11.25 litres). Squeeze the gooseberries by hand to express as much carbon dioxide gas as possible and add grape juice and orange juice. Stir and test for sugar. Add sugar to S.G. 1.086 approx. (6½ lb (3 kilos) used in test recipe). No acid was added as previous wines made with this fruit in this quantity were sufficiently acidic. Add pectin destroying enzyme, Bentonite and yeast nutrient and leave for a further two days when the must will be fermenting very vigorously. Strain and squeeze the fruit and transfer the fermenting liquor into gallon jars under airlock adding one Vitamin B1 tablet to each jar. Rack when fermentation has ceased (approx. three to four weeks if a reasonable temperature (65–70°F, 19–21°C) has been maintained), and again after a further four weeks when the wine should be very clear.

The addition of Bentonite will speed up the clearing process.

Damson (dry red table wine)

Ingredients to make 1 gallon (4.5 litres)

6 lb (2.75 kg) damsons
8 oz (250 g) packet dates
1¾ lb (875 g) sugar
2 level teaspoonfuls (5 ml size) tartaric acid
½ pint (300 ml) red grape concentrate
Pectin destroying enzyme
1 Vitamin B1 tablet (3 mg)
1 gram Kwik-Sol Bentonite (optional)
1 teaspoonful yeast nutrient
½ pint (300 ml) active yeast starter (Bordeaux or Burgundy)

Method:

Wash damsons and remove the stones. Place into the container with the dates, add ½ pint (300 ml) active yeast starter and seal. Stand in a warm place and leave to ferment for seven days. Transfer to sterilised fermentation bucket and add water to 7 pints (4 litres), sugar to S.G. 1.075 approx. and tartaric acid to 3.5 p.p.t. Add pectin destroying enzyme, Bentonite and yeast nutrient and leave for a further 2 days. Strain into gallon jar, add grape concentrate, 1 Vitamin B1 tablet and fit an airlock. Rack when fermentation has ceased (approx. 4 weeks) and again after a further 4 weeks when the wine should be clear. The addition of Bentonite speeds up the clearing process.

Peach (sweet white dessert wine)

Ingredients to make 1 gallon (4.5 litres)

6 lb (3 kg) peaches
½ lb (250 g) washed and chopped sultanas
½ lb (250 g) dates
2 lb (1 kg) sugar
½ pint (300 ml) white grape concentrate
2 heaped teaspoonsful tartaric acid
1 teaspoonful pectolase
1 teaspoonful nutrient
1 Vitamin B1 tablet (3 mg)
Active yeast starter (Madeira, Tarragona, Chateau d'Yquem)

Method:

Wash and stone the peaches and place into a suitable container (plastic sweet jar or plastic bag in a pressure cooker). Add sultanas, dates and ½ pint (300 ml) active yeast starter. Fix the lid tightly and if using a pressure cooker, the 15 lb weight and leave in a reasonably warm place (65–70°F, 19–21°C) for 7 days. Transfer to a sterilised bucket, add 6 pints (3 litres) cold water, sugar, acid, pectolase and nutrient and stir till the sugar is dissolved. Fermentation should be very active again within 2 days when the must can be strained. Add the grape concentrate and Vitamin B1 tablet and transfer to a gallon jar under airlock. Add sugar as necessary during fermentation to ensure maximum production of alcohol and rack when fermentation has ceased in 4–6 weeks and the wine sweet (S.G. 1.024–1.030 approx.).

Strawberry and Plum (medium sweet wine)

Ingredients to make 1 gallon (4.5 litres)

3 lb (1.5 kg) washed strawberries
3 lb (1.5 kg) washed and stoned plums
½ lb (250 g) washed sultanas
2 lb (1 kg) sugar to start
1 heaped teaspoonful tartaric acid
1 teaspoonful pectolase
1 teaspoonful nutrient
1 Vitamin B1 tablet (3 mg)
½ pint (300 ml) active yeast starter (Tarragona, Madeira or General Purpose)

Method:

Fill a plastic sweet jar with the fruit and add ½ pint (300 ml) active yeast starter. Screw the lid down tightly and leave in a warm place (70°F, 21°C) for 7 days. Transfer to a sterilised bucket and add sugar and cold water to make 1 gallon (4.5 litres). Stir till the sugar is dissolved and add pectolase and nutrient. Stir 2 or 3 times daily for 2 days then strain into a gallon jar under airlock, adding Vitamin B1 tablet.

Make further additions of sugar as necessary during fermentation and rack when fermentation has ceased in 4 to 5 weeks (S.G. 1.010–1.016).

Blackberry (sweet red wine)

Ingredients to make 1 gallon (4.5 litres)

6 lb (3 kg) blackberries
½ lb (250 g) dates
½ lb (250 g) washed sultanas
2 lb (1 kg) sugar to start
1 teaspoonful pectolase
1 teaspoonful nutrient
1 Vitamin B1 tablet (3 mg)
½ pint (300 ml) active yeast starter (Madeira or General Purpose)

Method:

Fill a plastic sweet jar with the fruit and add ½ pint (300 ml) active yeast starter. Screw the lid down tightly and leave in a warm place (70°F, 21°C) for 7 days. Transfer to a sterilised bucket and add sugar and cold water to make 1 gallon (4.5 litres). Stir till the sugar is dissolved and add pectolase and nutrient. Stir 2 or 3 times daily for 2 days then strain into a gallon jar under airlock, adding a Vitamin B1 tablet.

Make further additions of sugar as necessary during fermentation and rack when fermentation has ceased in 4–5 weeks (S.G. 1.026–1.030).

Greengage (sweet white dessert style wine)

Ingredients to make 1 gallon (4.5 litres)

5 lb (2.3 kg) greengages
8 oz (250 g) packet dates
8 oz (250 g) sultanas
1 rounded teaspoonful tartaric acid
2 lb (1 kg) sugar to start
½ pint (300 ml) white grape concentrate
Pectin destroying enzyme
1 Vitamin B1 tablet (3 mg)
1 teaspoonful yeast nutrient
½ pint (300 ml) active yeast starter (Tarragona, Madeira or Sauternes)

Method:

Wash greengages and remove the stones. Place into the container with the washed sultanas and the dates, add the active yeast starter and seal. Stand in a warm place and leave to ferment for seven days. Transfer to sterilised fermentation bucket and add water to seven pints (4 litres), sugar to S.G. 1.090 approx. and tartaric acid to 4.25 p.p.t. Add pectin destroying enzyme, and yeast nutrient and leave for a further 2 days. Strain into gallon jar adding grape concentrate and Vitamin B1 tablet. Fix an airlock.

Check the S.G. after 5–6 days and when it has dropped to 1.010 approx. add sufficient sugar to raise the S.G. to approx. 1.028 (See Chapter 1). Continue to feed the wine with sugar as necessary each time the S.G. reading drops to 1.010, the last addition of sugar, as fermentation is ceasing, being for sweetening purposes only. If a reasonable temperature has been maintained, (65–70°F, 19–21°C) fermentation will have ceased in about 5 to 6 weeks and about 16 to 17 degrees of alcohol by volume will have been achieved. Rack the wine from the lees and again after a further 4 weeks when the wine should be clear.

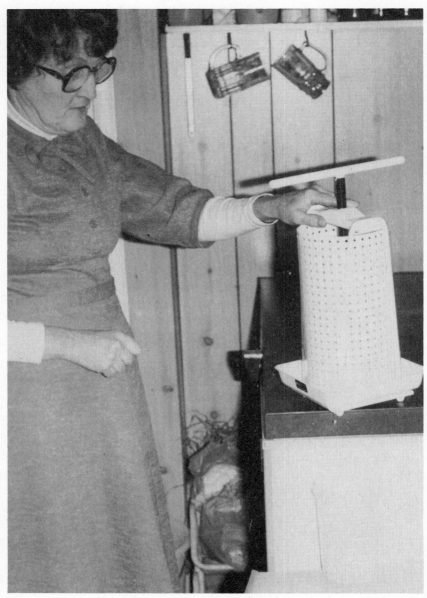

The Walker Desmond fruit press

Chapter 5

JUICE FERMENTATION

In the making of white wine from the grape, the commercial winemaker wants a clean, fresh, fruity wine and to ensure this, the wine is made from the juice of the grapes only. The grapes, after harvesting, are destalked, lightly crushed and then put into the wine press. The first juice expressed runs very freely and requires very little pressing due to the weight of fruit. In the very best vineyards this juice will be used to make a superior quality wine, the juice from the next pressing often going to make an ordinary "vin de table". In the smaller vineyards, all the juice collected is made into the one wine. Obviously then, over-pressing the fruit will bring disadvantages and in the amateur field we need to be doubly careful. The temptation to press or squeeze the straining bag to get more juice is something which needs to be resisted. Over-pressing can result in protein hazes which are difficult to clear.

Fermenting juice only has one obvious advantage. The juice can be tested accurately for natural sugar and acid and the necessary adjustments made before fermentation begins. There are many ways for the amateur winemaker to conduct a juice fermentation and it is a good idea to try as many as possible, compare the resultant finished wines, and decide upon the best method to use for each particular ingredient.

(i) Pressing

This seems the obvious choice, being the method used commercially, but it does pose problems for the amateur winemaker. Very few people are likely to own a wine press and buying even a small

The Moulinex Fruit Juicer

one can be quite expensive. To work efficiently they can only take a small amount of fruit at one time, and having literally to stand over it, one can get exasperated at the amount of time involved. It is necessary in the case of hard fruits like apples, gooseberries and rhubarb to cut the fruit up first into smaller pieces. Handpressing is only possible with soft fruits and even then a lot of juice will be left in the fruit pulp.

Protection of the fruit juice from oxidation needs to be considered and it is advisable to put some sulphite into the receiving vessel before pressing begins.

As the resultant juice is going to be treated in a similar manner to the next method of juice extraction, the fruit juicer, the recipes at the end of that section are suitable for both methods.

(ii) Fruit Juicers

Several winemakers may already have access to an electrical fruit juicer. Well-known brands of kitchen equipment have attachments for juicing and there is of course, electrical equipment specially for this purpose, i.e. the Vitamine or Moulinex.

A very good extraction of juice can be obtained in this way and, again, the main essential is to protect the juice from excessive browning by the addition of some sulphite to the receiving vessel.

Unfortunately, only a small amount of fruit can be processed at one time and it is necessary for this to be cut up reasonably small before feeding it into the machine. In some models, the juice is expelled from one outlet and the dry fruit residue from another, but in others, such as the Moulinex, the dry fruit pulp collects against the sides of the revolving drum. This necessitates cleaning the equipment several times during the juicing operation when a lot of fruit is to be processed.

Certain vegetables can be juiced and it is remarkable to see the amount of juice which can be obtained from carrots processed in this way.

Several firms are now marketing pure fruit juices and their relative cheapness makes one wonder if it is worth all the work and frustration in processing one's own. Without mentioning particular brand names, and there are several, shopping in the various Supermarkets and High Street stores can be very rewarding.

The juices most commonly found are apple, orange, grapefruit and pineapple and these are usually in lined cartons, date-stamped for recommended usage times. These juices can make some very nice wines although the flavour and aroma of the juice is not so appealing as for instance, the immediate taste and smell of freshly juiced apples.

It is essential when purchasing these juices, especially if one is trying a different brand, to read the small print on the carton. This, of course, applies to all fruit products purchased in tins, bottles or cartons. Quite often, manufacturers use sweetening agents, pre-servatives and artificial colouring and these can have a detrimental effect on the resultant wine. It is important to the winemaker to read on the label that the product has no added sweetness, colour-ing or preservatives.

Added sweetness may mean saccharine which will *not* ferment and, of course, does not register on the hydrometer either. A finished wine reading S.G. .990 but with a distinct degree of sweetness on the palate can often result from using products artifi-cially sweetened.

Added colouring can also be a problem and one particularly infamous experiment with a bottled blackcurrant juice resulted in a "WHITE" wine. The colour precipitated out of the wine as it was clearing after the first racking.

Added preservative may be a problem depending on the type and amount used in the process. Initial fermentation may be delayed and the yeast inhibited by its presence.

The following recipes have been used both with fresh fruit juice and with the commercially prepared product. The resultant wines in each case have been remarkably good.

Peach and Orange (sweet white wine)

Ingredients to make 1 gallon (4.5 litres)

Juice from 10 peaches (approx 1 pint (550 ml)
Juice from 10 oranges (approx 1½ pints (850 ml)
½ pint (300 ml) white grape concentrate
2 lb (1 kg) sugar
1 heaped teaspoon tartaric acid
1 teaspoonful nutrient
1 teaspoonful pectolase
1 Vitamin B1 tablet (3 mg)
Active yeast starter (Tarragona, Chateau d'Yquem)

Method:

Put the fruit juices, white grape concentrate and sugar into a sterilised bucket and add cold water to 1 gallon (4.5 litres). Stir till the sugar is dissolved and add acid, pectolase, nutrient and active yeast starter. Transfer to a gallon jar after 2 days, adding a Vitamin B1 tablet and fitting an airlock. Additional sugar may be added as necessary during fermentation to finish at S.G. 1.020–1.030.

Rack when fermentation has ceased in 4–5 weeks time.

White Grape (dry white table wine)

Ingredients to make 1 gallon (4.5 litres)

10–12 lb (4.6–6 kg) white grapes
1 lb 4 oz (625 grams) sugar
1 teaspoonful nutrient
1 Vitamin B1 tablet (3 mg)
Active yeast starter (Chablis or Burgundy)

Method:

Strip the grapes and wash in lightly sulphited water. Crush and press the grapes. Depending on the acidity of the grape juice, dilute with cold water to 4.25 p.p.t. and add sugar to S.G. 1.086.

Add nutrient and active yeast starter. Transfer to gallon jar after 2 days, adding a Vitamin B1 tablet and fitting an airlock.

Rack when fermentation has ceased in 3–4 weeks.

Grapefruit (dry white table wine)

Ingredients to make 1 gallon (4.5 litres)

2 pints (1 litre) grapefruit juice
2 pints (1 litre) white grape juice
1½ lb (750 grams) sugar
1 heaped teaspoonful tartaric acid
1 teaspoonful nutrient
1 teaspoonful pectolase
1 Vitamin B1 tablet (3 mg)
Active yeast starter (General Purpose)

Method:

Put the fruit juices and sugar into a sterilised bucket and add cold water to make 1 gallon (4.5 litres). Stir until the sugar is dissolved and add acid, pectolase, nutrient and active yeast starter. When actively fermenting add Vitamin B1 tablet and transfer to a gallon jar under an airlock.

Rack when fermentation has ceased in 3–5 weeks time when the wine should be dry (S.G. .992 approx.).

Seville Orange (dry white wine (aperitif style))

Ingredients to make 1 gallon (4.5 litres)

3 lb (1.5 kg) Seville oranges
½ pint (300 ml) white grape concentrate
2 lb (1 kg) sugar
1 level teaspoonful tartaric acid
1 teaspoonful pectolase
1 teaspoonful nutrient
1 Vitamin B1 tablet (3 mg)
Active yeast starter (Tarragona or General Purpose)

Method:

Peel the oranges and press the juice into a sterilised bucket putting the rinds (minus the pith) to steep in 2 pints (1 litre) of boiling water for 12 hours. Add sugar, nutrient, pectolase and cold water to 6 pints (3 litres) and stir till the sugar is dissolved. Strain the liquid from the rinds and add to the must along with the active yeast starter. Stir 2 or 3 times daily for 3 days, add grape concentrate and Vitamin B1 tablet and transfer to a gallon jar under airlock.

Rack when fermentation has ceased in 3 to 4 weeks and the wine is dry (S.G. .990 or below).

Apple (dry white table wine)

Ingredients to make 1 gallon (4.5 litres)

4 pints (2 litres) apple juice
2 pints (1 litre) white grape juice
2 lb (1 kg) sugar
1 heaped teaspoonful tartaric acid
1 teaspoonful pectolase
1 teaspoonful nutrient
1 Vitamin B1 tablet (3 mg)
Active yeast starter (Chablis, General Purpose)

Method:

Put the fruit juices and sugar into a sterilised bucket and add cold water to make 1 gallon (4.5 litres). Stir until the sugar is dissolved and add acid, pectolase, nutrient and active yeast starter. When fermenting actively add a Vitamin B1 tablet and transfer to a gallon jar under an airlock. Rack when fermentation has ceased in 3–5 weeks when the wine will be dry (S.G. .992 approx).

Apple and Orange (dry white table wine)

Ingredients to make 1 gallon (4.5 litres)

2 pints (1 litre) apple juice
2 pints (1 litre) orange juice
½ pint (300 ml) white grape concentrate
1½ lb (750 g) sugar
2 teaspoons tartaric acid
1 teaspoonful pectolase
1 teaspoonful nutrient
1 Vitamin B1 tablet (3 mg)
Active yeast starter (Burgundy, Chablis or General Purpose)

Method:

Sterilise a fermentation bucket and add apple juice, orange juice, grape concentrate, sugar and 2½ pints (1.25 litres) cold water. Stir till the sugar is dissolved and add acid, pectolase, nutrient and active yeast starter. Stir 2 or 3 times daily for 2 days then add Vitamin B1 tablet and transfer to gallon jar under airlock. Rack when fermentation has ceased and the wine is dry.

(iii) Steam Extraction

This method of extracting juice from fruit and vegetables by steam was first introduced into this country many years ago and has now become an established practice for many serious winemakers. The "Saftborn" is of German origin and although principally designed for sterilising juice for future use, the advantages it had for the winemaker soon became apparent. It is really a triple pan (see Fig. 1) and can be used on top of any cooking stove, electric ring or hot plate. It comprises a boiling pan, a perforated container for holding the fruit, a receptacle for collecting the juice, and a lid, all fitting neatly together. When in use, the steam from the boiling water in the bottom pan rises into the fruit "basket" and bursts the cell walls of the fruit, releasing the juice, which then drips down into the middle part of the Saftborn along with some condensed steam. The sterilised juice is then drawn off by means of the rubber pipe situated at the bottom of the collecting pan; this remains clamped during the extraction process. (See Fig. 2.)

Using a steam juicer.

The fruit is placed in the perforated basket.

There are many advantages in this method and perhaps the first that immediately comes to mind is the speed at which the fruit can be processed. It is unnecessary to de-stalk berries or remove stones from cherries or damsons, although it is advisable to remove large stones from fruits like plums, peaches and apricots. Hard fruits like pears and apples need to be cut into small pieces. Carrots and parsnips can also be "saftborned" but need to be cut up first.

The recommended extraction times vary for different types of fruit but for use in winemaking 35 to 40 minutes from the start of boiling time after layering the fruit with a little sugar is adequate.

There is a very good extraction of juice, normally about 6 pints (3.5 litres) from 14 lb (6.5 kilos) soft fruit. The large size Saftborn will hold this amount of fruit at one filling. In the case of elderberries a very good colour is maintained and the resultant wine appears to be mellower with a less harsh tannin content. There is no need to sulphite the juice if it is to be used immediately for it has been sterilised in the process and all micro-organisms have been destroyed. There is no risk of the juice tasting "stewed" or maderised as the fruit is never actually boiled. However, because it has been subjected to heat the soluble pectin level will rise and a pectin destroying enzyme should be added as soon as the juice is cool.

A double bonus is often achieved from fruit which has been through the Saftborn. Having used the juice to make a wine, the "pulp" can be used to make jam, marmalade or purées. With elderberries, some of the pulp residue can be packed into polythene cartons in the freezer and used as an additive when making a red wine which has not got a good depth of colour.

As many winemakers will appreciate, a lot of fruit is available at the same time and it is not always possible, due to lack of fermenting vessels and kitchen space, to process it all into wine at the same time. The Saftborn is a boon at this time as the sterilised juice can either be bottled for use on a future occasion or put into polythene cartons and stored in the freezer, taking up much less space than if the fresh fruit were frozen.

This extraction method is ideal for all red fruits and in the production of white dessert wines from fruits like peaches and apricots.

Elderberry and Damson (dry red table wine)

Ingredients to make 1 gallon (4.5 litres)

2½ lb (1.25 kg) elderberries
2½ lb (1.25 kg) damsons
½ lb (250 g) raisins
½ pint (300 ml) red grape concentrate
2 lb (1 kg) sugar
2 teaspoonfuls pectin destroying enzyme
1 teaspoonful yeast nutrient
1 x 3 mg Vitamin B1 tablet
Active yeast starter (Bordeaux or Burgundy)

Method:

Put the "saftborned" juice of fruit into the fermentation bucket with the washed and chopped raisins, sugar and cold water to approximately 7½ pints (4.2 litres). There is normally sufficient acid to give a titration of 4.0 p.p.t. so none need be added. Add pectin destroying enzyme, yeast nutrient and active yeast starter and ferment in the bucket for 4–5 days. Strain, add grape concentrate and Vitamin B1 tablet and transfer to gallon jar. Ferment in the normal manner and rack when fermentation has ceased.

Cherry and Blackcurrant (sweet red (dessert style))

Ingredients to make 1 gallon (4.5 litres)

4 lb (2 kg) Morello or dark red cherries
1 lb (500 g) Blackcurrants
8 oz (250 g) packet dates
1 lb (500 g) Muscatel raisins (washed and chopped)
½ pint (300 ml) red grape concentrate
1 level teaspoonful tannin
2 teaspoonfuls pectin destroying enzyme
1 teaspoonful tartaric acid
2 lb (1 kg) sugar to start
1 teaspoonful yeast nutrient
1 x 3 mg Vitamin B1 tablet
Active yeast starter (Tarragona or Madeira)

Method:

Saftborn the cherries and blackcurrants (fruit can be put through the Saftborn and the juice stored in the freezer until other fruits are available for blending) and put the juice into the fermentation bucket with the dates and raisins, sugar and tannin and acid. Add water to 7 pints and pectin destroying enzyme, yeast nutrient and active yeast starter. Stir 2 or 3 times daily for 4–5 days then strain, add grape concentrate and Vitamin B1 tablet and transfer to gallon jar. Watch the fermentation and add ½ lb (250 g) sugar (see Chapter 1) each time the hydrometer reading drops to S.G. 1.010. The final addition of sugar, when fermentation has ceased and the first racking takes place, should be to S.G. 1.028–1.030.

Elderberry and Blackberry (dry red table wine)

Ingredients to make 1 gallon (4.5 litres)

3 lb (1.5 kg) elderberries
3 lb (1.5 kg) blackberries
½ lb (250 g) sultanas
2 lb (1 kg) sugar
½ pint (300 ml) red grape concentrate
1 teaspoonful pectolase
1 teaspoonful nutrient
1 Vitamin B1 tablet (3 mg)
Active yeast starter (Bordeaux or Burgundy)

Method:

Saftborn the two fruits separately and put the juice into a sterilised bucket. Add ⅓ of the elderberry residue (to give additional "bite"), sugar, sultanas and cold water to 1 gallon (4.5 litres). Stir till the sugar is dissolved and add pectolase, nutrient and active yeast starter. Stir 2 or 3 times daily for 4 to 5 days then strain. Add grape concentrate and Vitamin B1 tablet and transfer to gallon jar under airlock.

Rack when fermentation has ceased in 4–5 weeks and the wine is dry (S.G. .990).

Peach (sweet white (dessert style))

Ingredients to make 1 gallon (4.5 litres)

4 lb (2 kg) peaches
2 lb (1 kg) ripe bananas, flesh only – no skins
½ lb (250 g) sultanas (washed and chopped)
½ pint (300 ml) white grape concentrate
2 lb (1 kg) sugar to start
2 teaspoonfuls tartaric acid
2 teaspoonfuls pectin destroying enzyme
1 teaspoonful yeast nutrient
1 x 3 mg Vitamin B1 tablet
Active yeast starter (Chateau d'Yquem, Sauternes, Tarragona)

Method:

Put the "Saftborned" peach juice and banana juice into the fermentation bucket with the sultanas and sugar. Add water to 7 pints and stir till sugar is dissolved. Add acid, pectin destroying enzyme, yeast nutrient and active yeast starter. Stir 2 or 3 times daily for 4–5 days. Strain, add grape concentrate and Vitamin B1 tablet and transfer to gallon jar. Add ½ lb (250 g) sugar each time the S.G. drops to 1.010 making the final addition of sugar when fermentation has ceased and the first racking takes place to raise the final S.G. to 1.028–30.

Elderberry and Peach (dry red table wine)

Ingredients to make 1 gallon (4.5 litres)

3 lb (1.5 kg) elderberries
2 lb (1 kg) peaches
½ lb (250 g) dates
½ lb (250 g) washed and chopped sultanas
1 teaspoonful grape tannin
1 level teaspoonful tartaric acid
1½ lb (750 g) sugar
1 teaspoonful pectolase
1 teaspoonful nutrient
1 Vitamin B1 tablet (3 mg)
Active yeast starter (Bordeaux or Burgundy)

Method:

Saftborn the fruit and put the juice into a sterilised bucket with the dates, sultanas and sugar. Add cold water to make 7 pints (4 litres) and stir till the sugar is dissolved. When cool add pectolase, tannin, acid, nutrient and active yeast starter. Stir 2 or 3 times daily for 4–5 days then strain. Add the grape concentrate and Vitamin B1 tablet and transfer to a gallon jar under airlock.

Rack when fermentation has ceased in 3–4 weeks and the wine is dry (S.G. .990).

Elderberry, Blackberry and Blackcurrant (dry red table wine)

Ingredients to make 1 gallon (4.5 litres)

2½ lb (1.25 kg) Elderberries
1½ lb (750 g) Blackberries
12 oz (375 g) Blackcurrants
½ lb (250 g) dates
½ lb (250 g) raisins (washed and chopped)
1½ lb (750 g) sugar
½ pint (300 ml) red grape concentrate
1 teaspoonful pectolase
1 teaspoonful nutrient
1 Vitamin B1 tablet (3 mg)
Active yeast starter (Bordeaux or Burgundy)

Method:

Saftborn the fruit (the elderberries separately from the other two fruits), and put the juice into a sterilised bucket with the elderberry residue, dates and raisins. Add cold water to make 7 pints (4 litres) and sufficient sugar to raise the specific gravity to 1.080 (1½ lb (750 g) sugar approximately depending on the natural sugar from the fruits). When cool add pectolase, nutrient and active yeast starter. Stir 2 or 3 times daily for 4–5 days then strain. Add the grape concentrate and Vitamin B1 tablet and transfer to a gallon jar under airlock.

Rack when fermentation has ceased in 3–4 weeks and the wine is dry (S.G. .990).

(iv) Freezing

When one first becomes the owner of a freezer it is not usually with the thought of its advantages in Winemaking, but rather for the economy of bulk buying, preserving garden produce and for the convenience of always having meat and vegetables available even when guests arrive unexpectedly. The books available to assist in using the freezer efficiently and to advise on freezing techniques always recommend fast freezing for the best results and to preserve the maximum flavour in the food.

For the winemaker there is another advantage, that of freezing and then thawing to cause the deliberate destruction of cellular tissue. Anyone who has used frozen strawberries will know what happens when the fruit thaws. If they are left too long the strawberries disintegrate into a mush and the juice is running freely. This would appear to be the ideal situation to reach with fruit intended for a juice fermentation.

When fruit, meat or vegetables, etc. are put into the freezer the liquid content freezes into sharp particles of ice which rupture the cellular tissue. In fast freezing, the particles of ice are small, so causing less damage to the cellular structure, but when one freezes slowly the ice particles are larger and a greater destruction will occur.

Bearing this in mind, the fruit should first of all be put into two or three thicknesses of polythene to help slow down the freezing process, and then placed in the freezer away from the fast freeze compartment.

All the soft fruits (strawberries, raspberries, blackcurrants, loganberries) release their juices very quickly and if the 'pulp' is put into a sieve or nylon straining bag it can be washed through with cold water to extract any remaining juice. Rhubarb is particularly good and needs to be cut into small lengths of about 4 inches before freezing. After thawing extra juice can be obtained by squeezing by hand. Marrow also should be cut into pieces after scooping out the seeds and removing the outer rind.

Apples, crab apples and quinces can be frozen whole and then squeezed by hand or in a straining bag. Quinces are particularly easy to handle after they have thawed and it is very easy to separate the flesh of the fruit from the bag of seeds in the middle.

Elderberries, blackcurrants and damsons can be frozen with equal success but there is a slight loss of colouring in red fruits. For this reason it is often preferable to pulp ferment or use steam extraction for red wines if an extra good colour is to be achieved.

Also on the credit side, freezing reduces the pectin level in fruit and this is a boon to winemakers, but perhaps explains why, in the making of jam the fruit doesn't set so easily.

Vitamin B1, which is vital for yeast growth, is unaffected by the freezing process but there is a slight loss of ascorbic acid (Vitamin C) so it is essential that sulphite is added as the fruit begins to thaw to act as an anti-oxidant.

One other point in favour of the freezing technique is, of course, the increased juice yield. More juice is obtained from freezing and thawing than by any other method.

Rhubarb and Orange
(dry white table wine)

Ingredients to make 1 gallon (4.5 litres)

1½ lb (750 g) rhubarb
Juice of 6 oranges
½ pint (300 ml) white grape concentrate
1 teaspoonful tartaric acid
1½ lb (750 g) sugar
1 Campden tablet or 5 ml sulphite solution
1 teaspoonful pectin destroying enzyme
1 teaspoonful yeast nutrient
1 x 3 mg Vitamin B1 tablet
Active yeast starter (Johannisberger, Bernkasteller or General Purpose)

Method:

Squeeze the thawed rhubarb into the fermentation bucket containing 2 pints of cold water and 5 ml sulphite solution. Add orange juice, grape concentrate, sugar and acid and cold water to 1 gallon (4.5 litres). Add pectin destroying enzyme, acid, yeast nutrient and active yeast starter, and stir 2 or 3 times daily for 2 days. Transfer to gallon jar adding the Vitamin B1 tablet. Ferment in the normal manner and rack when fermentation has ceased.

Rhubarb and Raspberry (rosé wine – dry)

Ingredients to make 1 gallon (4.5 litres)

1½ lb (750 g) rhubarb
1 lb (500 g) raspberries
¼ pint (150 ml) white grape concentrate
¼ pint (150 ml) red grape concentrate
1 teaspoonful tartaric acid
1½ lb (750 g) sugar
1 Campden tablet or 5 ml sulphite solution
1 teaspoonful pectin destroying enzyme
1 teaspoonful yeast nutrient
1 x 3 mg Vitamin B1 tablet
Active yeast starter (Bordeaux or General Purpose)

Method:

Squeeze the thawed rhubarb into the fermentation bucket containing 2 pints of cold water and 5 ml sulphite solution. Add juice from the thawed raspberries extracting as much juice as possible by "washing" the fruit in a sieve with 1 pint cold water. Add grape concentrate, sugar and acid, and cold water to 1 gallon (4.5 litres). Add pectin destroying enzyme, acid, yeast nutrient and active yeast starter. Stir 2 or 3 times daily for 2 days and transfer to gallon jar, adding the Vitamin B1 tablet. Ferment in the normal manner and rack when fermentation has ceased.

Marrow (sweet white wine)

Ingredients to make 1 gallon (4.5 litres)

5–6 lb (2.5 kg) frozen marrow
1 lb (500 g) washed and chopped sultanas
½ lb (250 g) dates
2 lb (1 kg) sugar
3 heaped teaspoons tartaric acid
1 campden tablet
1 teaspoonful pectolase
1 teaspoonful nutrient
1 Vitamin B1 tablet (3 mg)
Active yeast starter (Sauternes or General Purpose)

Method:

Place the frozen marrow and the campden tablet into a sterilised bucket and leave to thaw. Squeeze the marrow to extract maximum juice and discard the pulp. Add washed and chopped sultanas, dates, sugar, acid and cold water to 1 gallon, and stir till the sugar is dissolved. Add pectolase, nutrient and active yeast starter. Stir 2 or 3 times daily for 4 to 5 days, then strain into gallon jar under airlock adding the Vitamin B1 tablet. Additional sugar may be added as necessary during fermentation if a sweet wine is required. The wine should be racked when fermentation has ceased in approximately 3 to 5 weeks.

Apple (dry white table wine)

Ingredients to make 1 gallon (4.5 litres)

1½ lb (750 g) crab apples
4½ lb (2.25 kg) mixed cooking and eating apples
1 litre unsweetened grape juice
1¾ lb (875 g) sugar
1 Campden tablet or 5 ml sulphite solution
1 teaspoonful pectin destroying enzyme
1 teaspoonful yeast nutrient
1 x 3 mg Vitamin B1 tablet
Active yeast starter (Chablis or General Purpose)

Method:

Prepare fermentation bucket with approx. 2 pints (1 litre) cold water and 5 ml sulphite solution. Press the juice from the thawed fruit into the sulphited water and add grape juice, sugar and pectin destroying enzyme. Add water to 1 gallon (4.5 litres) and add yeast nutrient and active yeast starter. It is not necessary to add acid as the titratable acidity of the must is 4.25 p.p.t. approximately. Transfer to a gallon jar after 2 days adding the Vitamin B1 tablet and ferment as normal, racking when fermentation has ceased.

Loganberry and Raspberry (dry rosé wine)

Ingredients to make 1 gallon (4.5 litres)

12 oz (375 g) frozen loganberries
6 oz (200 g) frozen raspberries
2 pints (1 litre) white grape juice
1 campden tablet
1 lb 12 oz (875 g) sugar
1 teaspoonful pectolase
1 teaspoonful nutrient
1 Vitamin B1 tablet (3 mg)
Active yeast starter (Chablis or General Purpose)

Method:

Put the frozen into a sterilised bucket with a campden tablet and 2 pints (1 litre) boiling water. When completely thawed, strain through a nylon sieve or straining bag, washing through with more water to extract maximum juice. Discard the fruit pulp. Add white grape juice, sugar and sufficient cold water to make 1 gallon (4.5 litres). Add pectolase, nutrient and active yeast starter. When actively fermenting, transfer to a gallon jar under airlock adding the Vitamin B1 tablet. Rack when fermentation has ceased in approximately 3 to 4 weeks, and again in a further 4 weeks when the wine should be clear.

Bilberry and Raspberry (dry red wine)

Ingredients to make 1 gallon (4.5 litres)

3 lb (1.5 kg) frozen raspberries
3 lb (1.5 kg) frozen bilberries
½ lb (250 g) dates
½ lb (250 g) washed and chopped sultanas
2 lb (1 kg) sugar
1 teaspoonful pectolase
1 teaspoonful nutrient
1 Vitamin B1 tablet (3 mg)
Active yeast starter (Burgundy, Bordeaux or General Purpose)

Method:

Allow the frozen fruit to thaw then strain the liquid into a sterilised bucket. Using a sieve, "wash" the fruit with sufficient hot water to make 7 pints (4 litres), and to extract as much juice and colour as possible. Discard the fruit pulp and add dates, sultanas and sugar to the hot liquid. Stir till the sugar is dissolved. When cool add pectolase, nutrient and active yeast starter. Stir 2 or 3 times daily for 4 to 5 days then strain into gallon jar under airlock, adding the Vitamin B1 tablet. Rack when fermentation has ceased in 3 to 4 weeks time.

(v) Simmering

This is not a good method to use with fresh fruit because of the flavour changes and increased pectin levels. Cooked or maderised flavours are easily produced and, except in those wines where a Madeira style is intentional, the resultant wine can be very disappointing.

Root vegetables are, of course, a different matter and it is necessary to simmer carrots, parsnips, beetroot, potatoes, etc in order to obtain the flavour from them.

Carrots and parsnips contain pectin and it is of interest to note that when they are cooked the soluble pectin can rise by almost 60%. Preventative measures need to be taken at an early stage to ensure that the finished wines do not have a haze due to the presence of pectin.

Very economical wines can be made by using the blanching water from vegetables being prepared for the freezer. Due to the short period of blanching time, usually 3 minutes, only a small amount of the flavour is extracted. However, when blanching large amounts of vegetables and using the same water for 3 or 4 batches, the flavour level of the blanching water is increased making it eminently suitable for winemaking.

Dried fruits, such as apricots, peaches and prunes are very expensive, but they can be very economical in winemaking if used with care.

They should first of all be steeped in boiling water for 24 hours and then simmered for 15 to 20 minutes. Using the strained liquid only, and by careful blending with other fruit juices (see Recipe "Apricot and Orange" page 93), many different flavoured wines can be produced.

The "cooked" fruit should not, however, be wasted and although cooks may wish to use these for puddings or jams, they can be added to other musts for additional body and flavour. If it is not convenient to use them immediately, they can be packed into margarine cartons and stored in the freezer until required.

Carrot and Hops (dry white wine)

Ingredients to make 1 gallon (4.5 litres)

6 lb (3 kg) washed carrots
1 oz (30 g) hops
2 lb (1 kg) sugar
½ lb (250 g) washed and chopped sultanas
3 heaped teaspoons tartaric acid
1 teaspoonful pectolase
1 teaspoonful nutrient
1 Vitamin B1 tablet (3 mg)
Active yeast starter (General Purpose)

Method:

Simmer the unpeeled carrots until tender and strain the liquid into a sterilised bucket, saving the carrots for use as a vegetable. If wished the carrots can be peeled (saving the peelings and tops and tails) and blanched for the freezer. The peelings, tops and tails can then be simmered in the blanching water for 15 to 20 minutes to obtain maximum flavour.

Simmer the hops in 1 pint (550 ml) of water for 30 minutes and add the strained hop water to the carrot water in the fermentation bucket. Add the sugar and sultanas and stir until the sugar has dissolved. Make up to 1 gallon (4.5 litres) with cold water and when cool add the acid, pectolase, nutrient and active yeast starter. Stir 2 or 3 times daily for 4 to 5 days and strain into a gallon jar under an airlock adding the Vitamin B1 tablet.

Rack when fermentation has ceased in 3 to 5 weeks and the wine is dry (S.G. .990).

Parsnip (sweet white wine)

Ingredients to make 1 gallon (4.5 litres)

6 lb (3 kg) parsnips (preferably after a frost)
1 lb (500 g) muscatel raisins (washed and chopped)
2 lb (1 kg) sugar
3 heaped teaspoonsful tartaric acid
1 teaspoonful pectolase
1 teaspoonful nutrient
1 Vitamin B1 tablet (3 mg)
Active yeast starter (Sauternes, Tokay, Tarragona)

Method:

Wash and cut up the parsnips and simmer until tender. Strain the liquid into a sterilised bucket (the cooked parsnips can be used in soups or as a vegetable) and add raisins, sugar and water to 1 gallon (4.5 litres). Add pectolase, acid, nutrient, and active yeast starter. Stir 2 or 3 times daily for 4 to 5 days then strain into a gallon jar under airlock adding the Vitamin B1 tablet. Additional sugar may be added as necessary during fermentation whenever the S.G. drops to 1.010 approx. Rack in 4–6 weeks when fermentation has ceased, finishing at S.G. 1.024–1.030.

Apricot and Banana (dry white wine)

Ingredients to make 1 gallon (4.5 litres)

½ lb (250 g) dried apricots
½ lb (250 g) dried bananas
½ pint (300 ml) white grape concentrate
2 teaspoonfuls pectin destroying enzyme
2 teaspoonfuls tartaric acid
1 teaspoonful yeast nutrient
1 x 3 mg Vitamin B1 tablet
2 lb (1 kg) sugar
Active yeast starter (Chablis or General Purpose)

Method:

Wash apricots and bananas well to remove any preservative, cut the apricots into small pieces and put them into a basin with the bananas and 2 pints boiling water to steep overnight. Simmer in a saucepan for 15 minutes and strain into the fermentation bucket, saving the fruit either for use in the kitchen or to add to another "brew" as additional body. Add grape concentrate, sugar and water to make 1 gallon (4.5 litres), stirring till the sugar is dissolved, then add the acid, pectin destroying enzyme, yeast nutrient and active yeast starter. Transfer to gallon jar after 2 days adding the Vitamin B1 tablet and continue the fermentation in the normal manner, racking when fermentation has ceased.

Peach and Apple (dry white wine)

Ingredients to make 1 gallon (4.5 litres)

½ lb (250 g) dried peaches
½ pint (300 ml) apple juice
½ pint (300 ml) white grape concentrate
2 teaspoonfuls pectin destroying enzyme
2 lb (1 kg) sugar
2 teaspoonfuls tartaric acid
1 teaspoonful yeast nutrient
1 x 3 mg Vitamin B1 tablet
Active yeast starter (Chablis or General Purpose)

Method:

Wash the peaches well to remove any preservatives, cut into small pieces and put into a basin with 2 pints of boiling water and leave to steep overnight. Simmer liquid and peaches in a saucepan for 15 minutes and strain into fermentation bucket, saving the fruit for later use in the kitchen. Add apple juice, grape concentrate and sugar and cold water to make 1 gallon (4.5 litres) stirring till all the sugar is dissolved. Add acid, pectolase, yeast nutrient and active yeast starter. Transfer to gallon jar after 2 days adding Vitamin B1 tablet and ferment in normal manner, racking when fermentation has ceased.

Apricot and Orange (dry white table wine)

Ingredients to make 1 gallon (4.5 litres)

½ lb (250 g) dried apricots
2 pints (1 litre) fresh orange juice
½ lb (250 g) washed and chopped sultanas
2 lb (1 kg) sugar
1 heaped teaspoonful tartaric acid
1 teaspoonful pectolase
1 teaspoonful nutrient
1 Vitamin B1 tablet (3 mg)
Active yeast starter (Chablis or General Purpose)

Method:

Wash the dried apricots in cold water, cut them into small pieces and cover with hot water to steep for 24 hours. Simmer for 15 to 20 minutes, then strain the liquid into a sterilised bucket, keeping the fruit for use in the kitchen or in a further brew. Add the orange juice, sultanas, sugar, acid and cold water to 1 gallon (4.5 litres). Stir until the sugar is dissolved. Add pectolase, nutrient and active yeast starter.

Stir 2 or 3 times daily for 4 to 5 days, then strain into a gallon jar under airlock adding the Vitamin B1 tablet.

Rack when fermentation has ceased in 3 to 5 weeks.

Celery Wine (white medium sweet wine)

Ingredients to make 1 gallon (4.5 litres)

4 lb (2 kg) celery
½ lb (250 g) washed and chopped sultanas
1 lb (500 g) demerara sugar
1 lb (500 g) white sugar
½ pint (300 ml) white grape concentrate
1 large lemon
1 heaped teaspoonful tartaric acid
1 teaspoonful pectolase
1 teaspoonful nutrient
1 Vitamin B1 tablet (3 mg)
Active yeast starter (Sauternes or General Purpose)

Method:

Wash the celery stalks, cut them into small pieces and simmer with the lemon rind (no pith) until tender (approximately 30 minutes). Strain the liquid into a sterilised bucket (the celery can be used in the kitchen) and add sultanas, sugar, lemon juice and cold water to 7 pints (4 litres). Stir until the sugar is dissolved. Add acid, pectolase, nutrient and active yeast starter. Stir 2 or 3 times daily for 4 to 5 days then strain. Add grape concentrate and Vitamin B1 tablet and transfer to a gallon jar under airlock. A further ½ lb (250 g) sugar may be added as necessary during fermentation for the wine to finish medium sweet (S.G. 1.010–1.016). Rack when fermentation has ceased in 4–5 weeks.

Chapter 6

PECTIN REDUCING ENZYMES AND ROHAMENT 'P'

PECTIN

I have made reference to the presence of pectin in fruit and vegetables and how the amount of soluble pectin in the must can rise due to the method of extraction used by the winemaker, so perhaps it would be advisable if I devote a little space to this subject.

There is some pectin present in all fruit, some fruits containing more than others, and it is the presence of the soluble pectin in fruits which enables jam to set. Whilst this is of importance to the jam maker it is detrimental in the making of wine.

Pectin levels depend on the ripeness of the fruit. As fruit ripens, or is stored, the amount of pectin present changes. There is also a change in the nature of the pectin. So in unripe fruit we have a high percentage of insoluble pectin which gradually changes to soluble pectin as the fruit ripens. Subjecting the fruit to heat also increases the soluble pectin level and unless protective measures are taken, wines made by methods involving heat may develop hazes which are very difficult to clear later on.

In order to break down the pectin an enzyme is added to the must prior to the addition of yeast. This enzyme is available to the winemaker from most Homebrew shops and usually comes under the labels of Pectolase, Pectozyme, Pectinol, Pectinex and from one well known High Street store, as a "Pectolitic Destroying Enzyme". With the exception of Pectinex which is a much stronger preparation, it is added to the must in the ratio of one teaspoonful per gallon. In the case of fruits which have been subjected to heat, i.e. either by the hot soak method, simmering or the Saftborn, it is advisable to add two teaspoonfuls per gallon.

Because the enzyme is destroyed by heat, it should only be added to a must after it has cooled. As the presence of sulphite will also mar the effectiveness of the enzyme, it is advisable to wait 24 hours after sulphiting the must before making the addition.

Another property of the enzyme is its ability to break down the cellular structure of fruit giving an increased juice yield.

ROHAMENT P

This additive is readily obtainable from most Homebrew shops and is often used to break down the cellular structure of fruit to obtain maximum juice and colour.

Added at the ratio of 1 rounded tsp to 4 lb of fruit and kept at room temperature with frequent stirrings for 24 hours, a good juice extraction is obtained. For greater juice extraction it is advisable to heat the treated fruit pulp to 150–160°F (66–77°C) before pressing.

For maximum extraction of colour, the suppliers recommend that the ingredients and added Rohament P should be heated to 104°F (40°C) and held there for 1 to 2 hours stirring frequently.

Whilst Rohament P does give a very good juice yield if used correctly, the problem of maintaining the right temperatures and heating the pulp to inactivate the enzyme before pressing makes other simpler methods of juice extraction more attractive.

Additionally, because of the very good breakdown of the fruits cellular structure, one can have problems on pressing the fruit with the very fine sludge that is often present.

INDEX OF RECIPES

GLOSSARY OF TERMS

Acetic Acid
: A bi-product of fermentation normally undetectable on the palate. Greater quantities are formed in a wine which has been exposed to the air allowing access to bacteria, giving a vinegary taste and smell.

Acetic Acid Bacteria
: Can obtain access to a wine at any stage of the fermentation process hence the need for strict hygiene. It is often carried by the fruit fly.

Ascorbic Acid
: Can be added to wines at racking or bottling times as an anti-oxidant.

Bentonite
: A fining agent for clearing hazes in wine.

Body
: A tasting term to describe the fullness or thickness of wine on the palate.

Campden Tablets
: Sodium or potassium metabisulphite in tablet form. One tablet normally contains about 450 mg and is the equivalent of 5 ml stock sulphite solution.

Carbon Dioxide
: The gas given off during fermentation.

Citric Acid
: The main acid in citrus fruits.

Ethyl Alcohol
: The alcohol produced naturally in fermentation.

Flowers of Wine
: A disease forming on the surface of wine in powdery flecks. When the wine is moved it will fall to the bottom of the jar bottle resembling small white flower petals, hence the name.

Glycerine
: A bi-product of fermentation which gives a smoothness to wine. Can also be added to a harsh wine to mask the astringency.

Hydrometer
: A chemical instrument for measuring the density of a liquid.

Lactic Acid
: A bi-product of fermentation. It is also present in greater quantities following a malo-lactic fermentation.

86

Lactic Acid Bacteria	Can be both beneficial and detrimental in a wine. One species causes the malo-lactic fermentation which can be beneficial in a dry wine. Another can cause oiliness or ropiness and other wine disorders.
Lees	The sediment on the bottom of jars or bottles after fermentation.
Maceration Carbonique	A method of juice extraction using carbon dioxide pressure.
Maderised	A tasting term used to describe a cooked or burnt flavour.
Malic Acid	The main acid in apples.
Malo-Lactic Fermentation	The result of a bacterial infection of the wine causing malic acid to be broken down to lactic acid.
Mannitol	If a malo-lactic fermentation takes place in a sweet wine, the bacteria will also attack the sugar, breaking it down to mannitol – a sugar with a bitter taste.
Methyl Alcohol	Is formed in the breakdown of pectin to GALACTONURIC acid and methyl alcohol and is toxic in large quantities.
Mousiness	A bacterial disorder in wine giving a nasty after taste.
Must	The prepared juice extract after the addition of yeast.
Nutrient	Food for the yeast to enable good growth.
Oxidation	A small amount of oxygen is necessary in the maturation of wines but if a wine is exposed to large amounts of oxygen it will oxidise giving a distinctive, unpleasant flavour and bouquet depending upon the degree of oxidation.
Pectin	One of the main components in the cellular tissue of fruit. When extracted in the juice it can give rise to a haze which may be difficult to clear if not broken down during fermentation.

Pectin Destroying Enzymes	These are present in all fruit in small quantities. However, if heat has been employed during the process of juice extraction, these will have been denatured and it is essential to add a small amount of a commercial preparation prior to fermentation.
Pectinex Pectinol Pectolase Pectozyme	Commercial preparations of pectin destroying enzymes.
pH Papers	Litmus papers covering a range from 1–6 to determine to the acidity of wines or musts. Not normally accurate enough for the average winemaker. Litmus papers within the range of 8–14 determine alkalinity, 7 being neutral.
Phenol Phthalein	Used as a colour indicator solution in the titration of musts or wines to determine total acidity.
Racking	The removal of wine from its deposit, usually by syphoning.
Rohament P	A commercial preparation which breaks down the cellular tissue of fruit giving a greater juice yield.
Saftborn	A steam juice extractor.
Sodium Hydroxide	A strong alkali. At a strength of N/10 it is used in the titration of musts and wines to determine total acidity.
Sodium Metabisulphite	A preparation which, when made into a solution with water, is used for sterilising equipment and musts prior to fermentation. Is also used as an anti-oxidant.
Specific Gravity	The density of a liquid when compared with water.
Spoilage Yeasts	Usually occurs in aerobic conditions and forms on the surface of a wine. If not treated it will convert the alcohol to carbon dioxide gas and water.

Stock Sulphite Solution	Sodium Metabisulphite in a water solution. See Recipe on page 6.
Succinic Acid	A bi-product of fermentation which aids in ester formation. Can also be added at the first racking to those wines which require at least two years maturation.
Sulphuric Acid	A very strong acid but in the measurement of acidity in musts and wines is used for comparison, i.e. as per sulphuric.
Tartaric Acid	The principal acid in ripe grapes.
Tartrate	The precipitation of cream of tartar. The crystals (ARGOLS) form in the bottom of the jar, or on the corks when wine bottles are stored on their sides, when wine is stored in a cool place.
Titration	The technique of determining the total acidity of a wine or must by using an alkali and a colour indicator solution to show the "end point".
Vinosity	A tasting term used to describe "wine" character or "grapiness".
Vitamin B1	Essential for yeast growth. Usually included in wine musts at the rate of 3 mg per gallon.

APPENDIX A
Juice Extraction – by Type and Ingredient

Wine Type	Ingredient	Maceration — Cold Soak	Maceration — Hot Soak	Maceration — Alcohol	Maceration — Carbonique	Pressing	Vitamine etc.	Saftborn	Freezing	Simmering
White Dry Fruit	Apples					✓	✓	✓	✓	
	Gooseberries	✓					✓	✓		
	Rhubarb	✓					✓			
	Grapes					✓	✓	✓	✓	
	White Currants			✓			✓	✓		
White Sweet Fruit	Oranges					✓	✓			
	Peaches		✓	✓			✓	✓	✓	
	Apricots		✓	✓	✓		✓	✓	✓	
Red, Dry and Sweet Fruit	Elderberries		✓	✓	✓		✓	✓		
	Damsons		✓	✓		✓	✓	✓		
	Sloes		✓	✓			✓	✓		
	Grapes		✓	✓	✓	✓	✓	✓		
	Cherries		✓	✓			✓	✓	✓	
	Black Currants		✓	✓	✓		✓	✓	✓	
	Blackberries		✓	✓			✓	✓		
Rosé	Raspberries		✓	✓	✓		✓	✓	✓	
	Loganberries		✓	✓	✓		✓	✓	✓	
Flower	Flowers (ex Dandelion and Burnet)			✓						
	Dandelion		✓							✓
	Burnet									✓
Vegetable	Carrots									✓
	Parsnips									✓

APPENDIX B

Method		Effect
Cold Soak	− (a)	Inability to check correctly natural sugar and acid
	− (b)	Oxidation problems to be overcome
	+ (c)	Useful for cereal wines
Hot Soak	− (a)	Increases pectin level
	+ (b)	Gives a quicker colour and juice extraction
Alcohol	− (a)	Inability to check correctly natural sugar and acid
	+ (b)	Good for flower wines
Maceration Carbonique	− (a)	Inability to check correctly natural sugar and acid
Pressing	+ (a)	Clean juice extraction
	− (b)	Oxidation problems to be overcome
	− (c)	Overpressing can result in unwanted flavours
Vitamine	+ (a)	Clean juice extraction with maximum juice
	− (b)	Oxidation problems to be overcome
Saftborn or Fruitmaster	+ (a)	A mellower extraction with less harsh tannin content
	+ (b)	Good colour maintained in red fruits
	− (c)	Increases pectin level
	+ (d)	Micro-organisms are destroyed
Freezing	+ (a)	Reduces pectin and tannin levels
	− (b)	Some loss of colouring
	− (c)	Loss of ascorbic acid (up to 60%)
	+ (d)	Vitamin B (vital for yeast growth) is unaffected
	+ (e)	Good breakdown of cellular tissue giving increased juice yield
Simmering	− (a)	High pectin level in extract
	− (b)	Results in more methyl alcohol than desired
	+ (c)	Useful for some root vegetables

APPENDIX C

THE HYDROMETER

Specific Gravity	Gravity	Amount of sugar in the gallon		Amount of sugar added to the gall.		Vol. of one gall. with sugar added		Potential % of Alcohol by Volume
		lb.	oz.	lb.	oz.	gal.	fl. oz.	
1.010	10		2		2½	1	1	0.9
1.015	15		4		5	1	3	1.6
1.020	20		7		8	1	5	2.3
1.025	25		9		10	1	7	3.0
1.030	30		12		13	1	8	3.7
1.035	35		15	1	0	1	10	4.4
1.040	40	1	1	1	2	1	11	5.1
1.045	45	1	3	1	4	1	13	5.8
1.050	50	1	5	1	7	1	14	6.5
1.055	55	1	7	1	9	1	16	7.2
1.060	60	1	9	1	11	1	17	7.9
1.065	65	1	11	1	14	1	19	8.6
1.070	70	1	13	2	1	1	20	9.3
1.075	75	1	15	2	4	1	22	10.0
1.080	80	2	1	2	6	1	23	10.7
1.085	85	2	4	2	9	1	25	11.4
1.090	90	2	6	2	12	1	27	12.1
1.095	95	2	8	2	15	1	28	12.8
1.100	100	2	10	3	2	1	30	13.5
1.105	105	2	12	3	5	1	32	14.2
1.110	110	2	14	3	8	1	33	14.9
1.115	115	3	0	3	11	1	35	15.6
1.120	120	3	2	3	14	1	37	16.3
1.125	125	3	4	4	1	1	38	17.0
1.130	130	3	6	4	4	1	40	17.7
1.135	135	3	8	4	7	1	42	18.4

APPENDIX D
WEIGHTS AND MEASURES

Trying to work out exact equivalents from imperial to metric is a formidable task. In the following tables the metric quantities have been rounded off; in some cases to the nearest 25 gram equivalent.

Weights

Imperial	Metric (approx gram)
⅛ oz (1 level tsp)	5 g
¼ oz (1 heaped tsp)	10 g
1 oz	30 g
2 oz	60 g
3 oz	100 g
4 oz	125 g
8 oz	250 g
12 oz	375 g
1 lb	500 g
2 lb	1 kg
3 lb	1.5 kg
5 lb	2.3 kg

Measures

Imperial	Metric (approx)
¼ pint (5 fl oz)	150 ml
½ pint (10 fl oz)	300 ml
1 pint (20 fl oz)	550 ml
2 pints (40 fl oz)	1 litre
2 quarts (80 fl oz)	2.25 litres
1 gallon	4.5 litres

Temperature

Fahrenheit	Centigrade	Centigrade	Fahrenheit
212	100	100	212
100	37.8	35	95
80	26.7	25	77
70	21.1	20	68
60	15.6	15	59
50	10	10	50
40	4.4	5	41

INDEX

94

96

NOTES

NOTES

NOTES

NOTES

NOTES